Rush-hour Rider

Practical Horse-keeping for the Working Owner

PIPPA CUCKSON

THRESHOLD BOOKS

First published in Great Britain by
Threshold Books Ltd, 661 Fulham Road,
London SW6 5PZ
1989

British Library Cataloguing in Publication Data

Cuckson, Pippa
    Rush-hour rider: practical horse-keeping for
    the working owner.
    1. Livestock: Horses. Care, – Manuals
    I. Title
    636.1'083

    ISBN 0-901366-57-9

Illustrations by Dianne Breeze
Designed by Julia Lilauwala
Typeset by Rapid Communications Ltd, London, WC1
Printed in Great Britain by Hollen Street Press Ltd, Slough

Contents

Preface

The rapid growth of riding as a leisure pursuit in the past two decades has meant that a significant proportion of the country's horses are now cared for by 'first generation' owner-grooms. For many of them, leaving school and starting work provides their first opportunity to buy the horse or pony they so badly wanted as a child. Sadly, many people taking on a horse for the first time do not appreciate the extent of the commitment until it is too late. So often the fulfilment of their lifelong ambition becomes more of a penance than a pleasure.

Problems are considerable. 'Working novices', in particular, lack the practical knowledge that those with horsy parents have had drilled into them from the cradle. They invariably have to cope with the responsibility of a large, demanding animal either end of an equally demanding day in the office. And unless they have made enough money to buy the proverbial country cottage, horse-keepers with other jobs usually have the additional handicap of keeping the horse at a yard or rented premises away from home, travel to which puts further pressure on an already tight daily timetable.

When reading books on horse care I have often found myself frustrated by the assumption that the horse is on the doorstep, or that stable management is the reader's only responsibility. The idea of this book, therefore, is to supplement the wealth of sound knowledge available in many 'standard' horse-care manuals by suggesting ways of accommodating it in the working person's daily routine.

This does not mean that there are dozens of short cuts in keeping horses – if there were, the professional horse-keepers would surely have spotted them generations ago. However, there is much that can be done to avoid *creating* work. Certain tasks *can* be put off until the weekend without compromising the horse's welfare in any way, even if the purists might disapprove. And there is much, too, that can be done to minimise the time-consuming repercussions of accidents, or of the management problems peculiar to those who rely on others to provide a roof over their horse's head.

I have been a 'rush-hour rider' for over ten years, commuting not only to my job but to my horses as well. I hope that what I have learned will help new working owners to get as much fun out of their horses as I have, without walking into so many of the traps and wasting so much time.

Introduction

The horse is a complex, living machine and perhaps we tend to delude ourselves about how ideally it is suited to the physical and mental demands we make on it. The horse would have saved both himself and his owner a lot of trouble if he had evolved with the constitution, anatomy and personality of man's other two domestic animal friends, the dog and cat. How much easier it would be to have an animal which flourished on just one or two large, high-protein meals a day, could be taught to contain its excrement until directed outside by its owner, was able to keep itself fit, clean and healthy with a large amount of voluntary, strenuous exercise, and was self-sufficient enough to cope with long periods of boredom and its own company!

Regrettably that is far from the case. The horse, first identified as the fox-sized, herbivore called *Eohippus* 55 million years ago, has only been domesticated for about the last four thousand. This is a mere fragment of time in the evolutionary scale, and nothing like enough for him to even begin adapting to the new lifestyle we have imposed on him. It is a sad fact that the novice horse owner's ignorance of the fundamentals of horse psychology and physiology probably account for more horse-management problems than deliberate neglect. Certainly if everyone took the trouble to learn about the basic structure and function of the horse's limbs and vital organs he would know how to avoid physical problems that result in unsoundness, long lay-offs from work and expensive veterinary attention.

Although I did not acquire a horse of my own until I had finished my education and had started working at nineteen, I had at least ridden since the age of ten. I clearly recall that part of my lesson-time was always devoted to stable management and pony care. This invaluable knowledge was drilled into me from an early age, so that although I was a late starter in the horse-owning stakes at least I knew what to expect.

There is probably no justification for the next sweeping general-isation but I have a strong suspicion that adults taught to ride from scratch in today's booming leisure industry do not have the horse care aspect stressed nearly enough. This may well be because the adult learner is rather more aware of the value of money than is the child (it's different when your parents pay for you). He feels he is being 'ripped-off' if he doesn't spend every last second of his one hour on the horse's back.

But there comes a time when adult beginners want to buy their own horse, or at least do more with horses than be handed one to ride just once a week. This was brought home to me on a riding holiday overseas, when half of the British contingent comprised high-flying business executives and academics. Despite the fact that they had all been riding once a week for several years they were completely flummoxed when the tour guide announced that everyone would have to 'do' his own horse. At least the necessity for the more knowledgeable members of the party to demonstrate how to use a hoof-pick, tie a quick-release knot and tack up helped to break the ice on the first day!

Many distinguished persons have filled volumes on the subject of horse psychology and anatomy alone, so there is hardly room for such a dissertation in a book of this size.

The following notes on natural equine characteristics are, I must stress, very basic and limited to three main aspects – the herd instinct, exercise and digestion – but I hope they will go some way to explaining, especially to the new working horse owner, why horse care involves so many practices that appear unnecessarily pedantic. It is also hoped that they will encourage further reading elsewhere.

The nature of the horse

In its natural state the horse is a gregarious nomad, living in herds of varying sizes, never operating alone. He is a grazing animal, constantly on the move searching for food, grass being his staple diet. Obviously, as grass is of a low nutritive value, the horse needs to eat it in great bulk to keep himself nourished. His problem is that he has a relatively small stomach for his size – the average has a capacity of only 3.5 gallons (16 litres) – and thus it cannot be overloaded if the digestive juices are to work properly. To stop that happening, the horse's jaw is designed to take in quite small amounts at a time – rather like eating a steamed treacle pudding with a teaspoon – and thus by necessity he is eating almost round the clock. To extract every last bit of value from the food, the horse's intestines are by contrast extremely long – unravelled, the small intestine would stretch to a length of over 23 yards (21 m), and the large to 3.5 yards (3 m). One of the most crucial features of the intestine is that it narrows at various points and if it is not constantly serviced by a moderate flow of roughage, bits of food become impacted at these sites, ferment and form gases, which can lead to an attack of colic. Anyone who has ever sat up all night with a horse suffering from this severe digestive complaint will know why authoritative horse-keepers are so fastidious about feeding, for colic, so easily caused, can result in a twisted gut, and even prompt surgery is not always enough to prevent a fatality.

As his food intake comprises a high proportion of moisture, the horse in the wild or at grass drinks only twice a day, at dawn and dusk.

The horse may be built for speed, and able to perform great feats of athleticism when trained, but in the wild he is not naturally energetic or competitive. But his constant, steady movement keeps his muscles, wind and limbs in remarkably good trim and thus in readiness for his one great defence mechanism – escape. Except where rival stallions are concerned, the horse will not usually stand and fight when threatened – he gallops away. When safely out of danger he resumes his chief preoccupation – eating – and unless he is especially unlucky his limbs, muscles and organs have time to recover fully from the violent exercise before another predator forces him to stress them again.

Already one should begin to appreciate why domestication comes as such a shock to the horse. Just about everything we subject him to goes right against his nature. Really we are lucky that he is so tolerant. We deny his gregariousness by shutting him away from his friends for hours on his own. Maybe he even lives out of earshot of other horses. We take away his round-the-clock freedom of movement by keeping him in an area just big enough to turn round in, and even though we think we are being kind by turning him out in the field, in nature's terms he is still enclosed. Then we ask an animal indolent by nature to carry a significant extra weight at some speed, not just once in a while but several times a week, if not every day.

In our favour we recognise that to fulfil our athletic requirements day in, day out, we need to get the horse fitter than he would be from lolling about in the field (though how many of us, even full-time horse-keepers, can honestly say that they put in enough of the long, slow work that past generations knew was essential, to build the foundation for fitness?). We also understand that to fuel this requirement we must supplement his simple, natural diet with a more concentrated source of energy-giving and body-building nutrients. But then, again, every time we do the latter we are tampering with nature, for several times a day we throw his digestive juices into overdrive with a huge helping of solid food. And much of it is so dry that we then encourage him to drink copious amounts of water at times nature would say were wrong.

Old mottoes like 'feed little and often' and 'water before feeding', have been passed down the ages and indicate that our ancestors were well aware of the need to spread the feeding over the 24-hour period. Given that a horse can reasonably be expected to digest up to 5 lbs (2.2 kg) of concentrates in addition to his bulk feed every 4 hours, in practical, labour-saving terms this has resulted in the concentrate ration of the stabled horse being split into three, four or even five feeds a day, depending on the horse's size and volume of hard work.

The timing of these feeds forms the outline of the accepted stable-yard routine and its necessarily long working day. Generally speaking, yards caring for fit animals on a non-hunting or competition day would give the first feed of the day at about 7 a.m. As the horse cannot be ridden for at least 1½ hours after a full feed (principally because of the risk of upsetting the digestion and causing colic, but also because a swollen stomach will interfere with the efficiency of vital organs like the heart and lungs), the next 2 hours will be spent on stable work. This will include the main mucking out, changing water, giving a horse a quick brush-over and taking away his haynet in readiness for the ride. Exercise and schooling may then take place between 9 a.m. and 11 a.m. For the hour leading up to the second mid-day feed the horse might enjoy a thorough grooming (or strapping as it is known) for at least 30 minutes if he lives in full-time, and be allowed to pick at a small daytime haynet. He may then be turned out for a spell in the field for 3 to 4 hours after lunch. Mid to late afternoon the horse will be brought in before tea at about 4.30 p.m. and his main haynet which will last the night, while his fully stabled neighbour may have his rugs reset and his bed tidied up, or 'set-fair'. Then in the evening, at about 8 p.m., he would have his final feed, his hay and water topped up, his bedding skipped out and rugs readjusted for the long night ahead without human attention. In between these key tasks his groom would clean tack, fill up haynets, sweep and tidy the yard and manure heap, and see to a host of routine daily tasks, not to mention fitting in the farrier, maybe the vet, stacking a load of hay and many other time-consuming extra tasks that have to squeezed into a tight regime.

Observing the ground rules of horse-keeping clearly presents a great challenge for the working owner, maybe involving as much forward planning and as many decisions as your job. Even if you intend to get some help (which for most people is rarely much more than persuading a friend to give a lunchtime feed, or to bring in the horse at night to a stable containing the hay, feed and water that you have already set up), you are imposing a further radical change to the horse's daily regime by cramming an extensive list of tasks into two or maybe only one often hurried visits either end of the daylight hours.

It is a daunting prospect and a responsibility that should not be taken lightly. In the following chapters I hope to explain how it can be done.

Chapter 1

Expenses

Leaving school or college and earning money for the first time provides many riders with a long-awaited first opportunity to have a horse of their own. The irony then, however, is that even if they can afford to buy and run a horse, the average wage-earner cannot necessarily spare the time that enables him to maximise the use of the animal. Certainly there have been many winters when I have wondered why I spend two hours a day travelling to a better-paid job in London to be able to afford two horses that I cannot find the time to ride...

Adults going into horse-keeping with no previous experience must therefore decide not only whether they can afford it but also whether they can really *justify* the expense too. During the summer months, working riders can get real value from owning a horse by minimising chores and expenses through keeping it wholly or partly at grass and by having plenty of time to ride in the long evenings. Half the year round, however, in the winter months both chores and expenditure will double if not treble, and there will be scant opportunity to ride except at weekends.

Of course, for many people the pleasure of owning a horse is not just in the riding but also in the caring and companionship and the immense pleasure that can be gained from building up a relationship with an animal over the long-term. However, if you are interested in riding principally as a form of non-competitive exercise, it simply may not be cost-effective to own a horse. It could even be cheaper to go to a riding school and hire a horse for the number of hours' riding you can fit in after doing all the essential stable work.

However conscientiously you work out the figures, horse-keeping always costs more than you think and it is not exaggerating to suggest that you should double the figure you arrive at. Those without horse-keeping facilities at home or back-up assistance from knowledgeable friends or members of the family will have to pay for amenities and probably some labour. Charges and rental fees at livery yards and private farms and stables can vary widely even within localities, and they can be rife with hidden extras.

Horse owners, myself included, rarely sit down to work out the true cost of their hobby because they are terrified of discovering the truth. However, it is as well to go into the venture with your eyes open, for the horse's sake as much as your own. The novelty of horse-keeping can soon wear thin in the winter when you face feed bill after feed bill, arduous manual work in bad weather, and a constant battle against mud with little riding in return. For those whose whole social life does not revolve round equestrianism, other hobbies, evening activities and weekends away have to be planned like a military manoeuvre. There is often the added irritation of having to turn down last-minute invitations because you cannot find anyone to help out with the horse at short notice. One must have balance in life, and if everything is governed by horse-keeping commitments, the working owner can often find himself beginning to resent his unfortunate animal. Once this happens, chores start to be rushed or skimped and sloppy habits creep in. Why should the horse suffer just because the owner did not appreciate what a tie he would be?

Most people are inclined to write off the initial capital expenditures – the horse itself, tack, clothing and other equipment – and concentrate instead on regulars like livery charges, field or stable rental, hard feed, hay, bedding, shoeing, insurance and routine veterinary fees when working out the weekly costs. If, having done this, you feel you will be financially stretched then do think very seriously about whether or not you should go ahead with horse-keeping; the 'invisible' costs are horrendous, can encroach on all aspects of your life and can easily double the weekly cost in real terms.

These 'invisible' costs will include repair and replacement of equipment – rugs get ripped, haynets chewed, bootstraps broken and saddles want re-stuffing – which can add £200 in £5 and £10 units here and there to your annual bill. Then there are unscheduled visits from the farrier when your horse loses a shoe, the excess to pay on insurance claims for veterinary treatment – frequently £25 or £50 per claim – plus the cost of telephone calls to arrange them all.

For the rider there is the purchase of extra riding clothes and waterproofs that you would not normally need – an extra quilted

13

coat, maybe a second pair of jodhpurs and rubber boots – none of which come cheap.

Then, for the many who commute to their horses, there is the wear and tear on the car. Even if your horse is only 4 miles away, a twice-daily visit means a 16-mile round trip, totalling nearly 6,000 miles' worth of fuel and 6,000 miles on the clock a year. An accountant friend who keeps a horse estimates that her hobby adds an extra 25 per cent to the annual depreciation of her car.

If you consulted an accountant professionally he would take the analysis of the true cost even further. He would point out what your money would have earned if it had been invested as a lump sum instead of being frittered away on the horse and its related expenses.

The self-employed person should also consider the extra income he could have earned in the time spent on stable chores. Even if you argue that grooming and tack cleaning are part of the fun, the DIY horse-keeper could spend two hours a day on menial chores for the stabled horse. Some horse-keepers may find that their other skills could have earned rather more than the £3 or £4 an hour that it costs to hire a freelance stable-hand to shovel muck (and there are quite a few self-employed girl Fridays about these days who are willing to do just that, the use of which will be discussed later).

When all these invisible costs are taken into account the prospective DIY horse owner may find it is just as economical to have his horse at full livery after all and to use the time saved either enjoying extra riding or earning money to pay the bills.

As no two individuals' circumstances are the same it is invidious in just one chapter to attempt to advise horse-keepers exactly how to manage money. Only the individual knows where he wants to make the dividing line between buying the services of others to make more time for himself, or sacrificing his time to do the work that saves the money.

The system that has worked for me, after learning the hard way over several years, is to work out a realistic monthly budget, taking into account all the hidden extras mentioned above, and then to open a special 'horse' account at the bank, for which I deliberately did not request an overdraft facility. My salary is paid monthly into my main account and I immediately transfer a seasonally adjusted, monthly sum into the secondary horse account. I then strive to keep my equestrian expenditure within it. Of course there are occasions when I have to dig into other funds, such as when a New Zealand rug is ripped beyond repair, or if I have emergency veterinary fees not immediately recoverable from the insurance company. But the discipline of keeping this account in the black and the separation of horse expenses from domestic ones keeps me continually aware of where economies could be made. I think twice before buying a new item of tack or trying out an expensive new feed supplement (which in all probability won't make any noticeable different to my horses' well-being).

The second factor is to make a strict resolution not to buy anything equestrian using a credit card; I have a chest full of hardly used, unnecessary rugs, sheets, bits and boots that have been bought on a whim over the years thanks to the cursed plastic.

Chapter 2

Systems of horse-keeping

There are numerous means of keeping a horse. They range from the cheapest – having the horse at home and doing all the work yourself either end of the working day – to the most expensive – putting your horse at full livery. Those opting for these two systems have the least interest in this book: the former because they do not have the considerable handicap of having to travel to the premises where the horse is kept and who in many cases will have back-up help from members of the family while they are at work; and the latter because the horse-owner has no responsibility for the management of his horse at all, merely turning up to ride when he feels like it and having to do nothing more strenuous than writing out a cheque at the end of the month.

The average working person is most likely to have to keep the horse away from home and will opt for a compromise – the part-DIY system at a commercial or semi-private yard. This is the system to be most heavily featured in this book. There are many alternatives, however, so here they are outlined, starting with the cheapest and working through to the most costly, discussing the advantages and disadvantages, relative costs and the lifestyles to which they are best suited. The suggested weekday time commitment should be taken in all cases as a bare minimum merely to attend to the basic needs of the horse. The less you do, for instance, to keep your bedding up to scratch during the week, the more work you create for yourself at weekends.

Keeping the horse at home

If you live in a rural area and have stabling and grazing at home it is unlikely that you are the only member of the family interested in horses. You may already be so experienced in keeping horses that coping with the horses round a full-time job requires only minor modifications to your regime.

16

There is no reason why the suburban resident should not put up a stable in his back garden, however small that garden may be; it is commonly assumed that planning regulations are automatically against this. In fact, you do not have to apply for consent if you are building a stable as an extension to your house and if total extensions do not exceed 10 per cent of the cubic area of the *original dwelling*.

Brick buildings look nicer but are expensive and will not necessarily add to the value of the suburban residence. On the other hand, even an economy timber box can look aesthetically pleasing in an urban area and, with adjoining feed and tack shed, will pay for itself in about a year to eighteen months (slightly longer if you also have to put down hard-standing) when compared with the cost of renting the same type of box from a livery yard. You thus have the advantage of keeping your horse 'rent-free' after the initial capital outlay is recouped, and the opportunity to take the boxes with you or sell them if you move house.

The disadvantages for the suburban horse is going to be lack of turn-out, which obliges the owner to ride for at least an hour, and preferably two, a day, and it means you must have ample hacking, even on quiet suburban roads, nearby. Ideally, the stabled horse whose morning exercise is limited by his owner's working hours should also have some leg-stretching activity for a short period in the evening, which is a very heavy commitment indeed for the working owner. Problems come in periods of bad weather when you cannot get out to ride and the horse is literally holed-up for weeks; without even a play-patch to roll in and scamper round, his metabolism and temperament will be adversely affected. You will need to be able to call on a knowledgeable friend to look after the horse when you are away (it is hardly as simple as asking a neighbour to pop in and feed the cat), and, of great importance, your horse will be lonely for the greater part of the day.

Even if you don't fall foul of the local planning authority, your horse-keeping could come to the attention of the environmental health department. A large muck-heap is out of the question, so unless you are surrounded by keen gardeners you will have to find a way of moving manure and soiled bedding out of the locality; access for tractors and other heavy vehicles is therefore another consideration. If you cart it away yourself it is an extra weekend chore; if you have to pay someone else to do it, there is another hidden expense. Vermin can also be a problem. The idea of putting down poison in a residential area where there are a lot

17

of pets, may be out of the question. Some other vermin deterrents – such as small battery-operated units which frighten off rats and mice by emitting a high-pitched noise – are now on the market, but at a price.

A further problem for the suburban horse-keeper is likely to be lack of storage space. He will not be able to take advantage of buying hay in bulk straight off the field at a discount, or cheap shavings, and will thus have to buy them in small quantities from feed merchants, thus increasing costs and travelling time.

Unless you have previous practical experience of horse-keeping I would not recommend that you keep your first horse at home. It may be cheap but you will not have the buffer of experienced advice that is usually available from the proprietor or fellow clients at livery yards.

SUITABLE LIFESTYLES: Any kind of job within spitting distance of home, enabling return at lunchtime where necessary and with regular hours, not involving the owner in staying away from home unless he has the wherewithal to employ occasional freelance help.

SUITABLE HORSES: Cold-blooded, less high-couraged horses will generally but not always cope better with long periods of stabled boredom or loneliness. Owners will need to give their horses interesting pre-office hacks, a good strapping in the evening and busy weekends to keep the mind and circulation right.

WEEKDAY TIME COMMITMENT: Stable work – a.m. 45 minutes, p.m. 45 minutes; plus exercising.

Field and/or stable rental (field and stable rental often run in conjunction)

The owner rents a field and/or buildings direct from a farmer or landowner at rates usually lower than paying for use of such facilities at a yard or riding school catering for many clients. The advantages are that you are your own boss and can have exclusive use of the field, with freedom to manage the pasture as you would wish, with no worries about other people or their horses interfering with your own. You will be able to make storage space and thus take advantage of bulk-buying hay and bedding, unlike the owner described above.

The disadvantages are considerable and all stem from the absence of the word 'livery'. When you rent a field you are paying for a facility, not a service, and thus responsibility for the horse falls to you entirely. You must attend to his every need 7 days a week, 52 weeks a year, come rain or shine, and should not attempt any such arrangement unless you have already secured the back-up help of family and friends in the event of your inability to attend due to sickness or delays at work. It would be a hard-hearted farmer who did not bother to 'phone you at work if he spotted your horse in difficulties, but he is under no obligation to do so, nor to help you with late-night feeds or hay if you are unavoidably delayed. For this reason, it is advisable to rent a field big enough for two horses and either share or sub-let grazing to a friend. You can then help each other out and, more importantly, your horses will have that valuable companionship that helps to keep them happy for the 22 hours of the day when you are not with them.

Further disadvantages include hidden expenses, such as having to pay rental many months in advance – and the risk of losing that money if you wish to move because the arrangement has not worked out.

Responsibility for maintenance of fencing and buildings will also fall to you, as does management of grazing. Most horse owners welcome the opportunity to control the latter but the cost of hiring a tractor and/or driver to harrow, roll and top pasture is an extra expense.

There may be restrictions, too, on the way the field is used. If you rent a field that has always been grazed, and want to put down a rudimentary manège or a set of jumps, the local authority may argue that this constitutes a change of use for which planning consent may not necessarily be forthcoming. The chances of the latter have increased in recent years in semi-rural and suburban areas where local authorities have been acutely aware of the visual blight of 'horsiculture'. Local authority interest may often depend on a local busy-body 'splitting' on you. The decision about whether to draw the authority's attention to your activities is up to the individual after discussion with the farmer or landowner, who will take a dim of view of the possibility of having to pay extra rates on non-agricultural use of his amenities; he will undoubtedly want to pass such extra costs on to you. In my work as a journalist I have encountered several planning stories of this nature. One of these involved a man who, in the course of getting his horse fit, had regularly cantered round the edge of a field which was also used for grazing. He incurred the wrath of the planning authority when he advertised the fact by laying a shavings track (at a cost of thousands

19

of pounds) round that same boundary to guarantee the going in all weathers. He was served an enforcement notice on grounds of unauthorised change of use and unsuccessfully appealed against it, at further expense.

The aspect of isolation, security and safety of both horse and owner also warrants special consideration in the case of field rental. A horse kept in a field miles from anywhere is more at risk to theft, or to be left unnoticed for hours if he is unwell or has managed to injure himself, or has even escaped. If the owner is late home, how is anyone to know whether he has simply stayed late at the field to do some mane-pulling or to catch up on tack cleaning, or whether it is because he or she has had an accident and is unable to summon help? Sadly, in this day and age of prowlers and molesters, it also has to be stressed that it is not safe for females of any age to be on their own out of earshot in isolated rural spots. Again, the novice horse-keeper has no one to consult when minor problems occur.

SUITABLE LIFESTYLES: In view of the above and the heavy burden of responsibility, field rental can only be recommended for those who live and work no more than a mile or two away, are able to return at lunchtime if necessary, and have a supply of reliable friends or relations who can help in emergencies.

SUITABLE HORSES: As before.

WEEKDAY TIME COMMITMENT: Stable work – a.m. 45 minutes, p.m. 45 minutes; plus exercising and travelling.

Grass livery

Here the owner rents *use* of grazing from a yard or farm. Instead of having exclusive use of a field, the horse is more of a paying guest and the owner will not necessarily have any say in which field his horse is turned out, or with how many horses he has to share it. The proprietor usually accepts responsibility for maintenance of grazing, fences, gates and the water supply and has a moral obligation to keep a watching brief over the animals on his property and help out in emergencies. As a rule, for an extra weekly payment he will put hay out in the winter for all the horses. This generally works well but can present problems if the owner does not approve of the quality of hay offered. It can also mean that the owner has to time his evening rides or after-hours competitive activities carefully if the horse is not to miss his important bulk evening feed. Hard feeding all the year round falls to the individual. This can only be satisfactorily managed if the proprietor provides a barn, enclosure or other tying-up area for the grass liveries who are not paying for use of a box. Trying to feed your horse in a field with others looking on and trying to get in on the act is a nightmare; it is unkind to the other horses, while your own horse, feeling intimidated, may bolt his food, which can cause digestive problems and even colic. Again, unless the grass livery is attached to some sort of stable yard there may be nowhere for the owner to store feed or even basic items of equipment, and your car will soon become a mobile feed store and tack shed.

SUITABLE LIFESTYLES: As the above two systems. Possible, but miserable and often frustrating winter system for anyone with aspirations to do anything competitive or more demanding than hacking out at weekends, due to the difficulties of managing diet and fitness and keeping the horse clean.

SUITABLE HORSES: Any in the summer as long he is not expected to do anything more strenuous than hacking, dressage or show jumping at weekends. Not suitable for better bred or 'blood horses' in the winter, or anything clipped more drastically than a low trace, even if rugged; such horses must come in at night or else they will lose condition far quicker than you can put it back on.

WEEKDAY TIME COMMITMENT: Summer – morning check, 10 minutes; evening grooming, tacking up and feeding, 30 minutes; plus riding and travelling time. Winter – morning check, feeding, re-turn-out and grooming time 30 minutes; evening feed, rug straightening, etc. 20 minutes; plus travelling and riding time.

The timings are subject to more variation than in systems where horses are stabled due to the possible long distance of the field from the stable and/or tacking-up area, and the problems that arise when (and if) the horse refuses to be caught.

DIY stabled livery

Here the horse-keeper rents the stable, use of grazing and other facilities from a riding school, commercial livery yard or semi-private establishment, and undertakes to do all the work himself, seven days a week. For those without stables or grazing at

21

home this is preferable to renting an isolated field or buildings for you keep the costs as low as possible while enjoying the company and support of others. However, as with the above two systems the entire responsibility of looking after the horse falls to you and you may be involved in a lot of travel to boot. At straightforward DIY yards the proprietor will probably keep a watching brief over the horses and help out in emergencies; he should also accept responsibility for maintenance of stables, fields and gates and the water supply.

Usually in these circumstances horse owners pal up with others at the yard in the same circumstances and help each other out. This ensures slightly greater freedom and the assurance that your horse will not go unattended if you are unavoidably delayed. However, you should not assume this arrangement when moving to a new yard and must be prepared to do all the work yourself.

Generally you are provided with facilities to store tack and your own equipment and you can provide your own hard feed or buy it direct from the yard, which saves time. Unfortunately, you often feel obliged to buy your hay and bedding direct from the yard which can be awkward if you do not like the quality on offer.

SUITABLE LIFESTYLES: As for keeping a horse at home or in field or stable rental, although those working irregular hours or a lot of overtime may be able to persuade others at the yard to help out.

SUITABLE HORSES: Any. Fit competition animals and other higher couraged types will do better in this sort of yard than those kept in isolation at home due to the company of other horses and the scope for extra attention.

WEEKDAY TIME COMMITMENT: As for keeping a horse at home, plus travelling and riding time.

Part-DIY livery

A development of the above, giving the owner the best of both worlds. He rents facilities at a commercial yard and does most of the chores himself, simply paying the yard to do those he cannot manage. For the working owner, this will normally include the bringing in of the part-stabled horse from the field in the evening, rugging up and giving feeds that you have left prepared. The advantages are that it keeps the owner's expenses to the minimum, enables him to see exactly how his money is spent and gives the satisfaction of knowing his horse is being attended to when he is unavoidably delayed. (In my experience, although creatures of routine, stabled horses don't mind whether you turn up to see them for extra late-night attention at seven o'clock or midnight as long as they come in for tea and have their haynet at the same time as the other horses.) Of greater reassurance, the proprietor is also committed to paying more attention to his charges. If you leave everything prepared for the yard in the evening, an early start does at least compensate you with no obligation to attend the horse again at night. However, a mornings-only visit cannot be recommended if the yard does not supply a late-night stables service for all its clients; a stabled horse should not go unattended from, say, 5 p.m. until 7 or 8 a.m. the next day.

Disadvantages are that costs and services can vary considerably. You may find you have to pay extra for the use of amenities like manèges or show jumps. There may be a standard payment of provision of feed when you feel you could provide it cheaper yourself. In addition, although the yard may be happy to do emergency mucking out for you at a price, it may not in turn offer you a discount if you are able to do all your stable duties on days off or public holidays. These are perhaps minor irritations, however, and overall, the part-DIY system offers the budget-conscious owner and his horse the best deal.

Further advice on choosing a DIY or part-DIY livery yard is offered in Chapter 3.

SUITABLE LIFESTYLES: Suitable for the owner who likes to dictate the management of his horse and have some direct involvement with it, and who wishes to save money and yet have time for other hobbies. Ideal for those who work regular hours but have a longish journey to work and who are at the mercy of public transport, because with this system they can usually rely on evening help when delayed.

SUITABLE HORSES: Any, as one has guaranteed extra help, supervision and the provision of company for the horse. Particularly suitable for those preparing animals for competition as they have 'bought' that little bit extra riding time by paying to have some of the time-consuming chores done for them, and the extra help enables the diet to be managed accordingly.

WEEKDAY TIME COMMITMENT: Assuming one visit daily, 75 minutes stable work a.m., including preparation of night-time feeds etc., plus travelling and riding time.

23

Working livery

Also known as part livery and thereby open to some misunder-standings, this system is often offered by commercial riding schools. The owner has his horse looked after entirely by the establishment as a full livery, but he pays a discounted fee. In return for this, the school has use of the animal for an agreed number of hours per week. The advantages are that, if placed at a good British Horse Society or Association of British Riding Schools approved centre with a reputation for training students for recognised qualifications, your horse may benefit from being schooled by a competent student under expert supervision. He will also be fitter than you could probably get him in your own time, for which reason it will be much easier for the working owner to entertain the idea of hunting or other cross-country work during the winter. The disadvantages are that, at a lesser establishment, you may not have much say over the competence of the rider to be put on your horse. Inevitably, too, the yard will have most need of your horse at the weekends which is also, of course, the time when you want to ride. There can also be problems over insurance. Most companies charge an extra premium for the cover of horses used in riding schools. Even if yours is only used two hours a week in controlled conditions it may fall into this category.

SUITABLE LIFESTYLES: Any but especially useful for those on shift work, those whose job takes them away from home overnight or those who have to work weekends.

SUITABLE HORSES: Useful for keeping any kind of animal extra fit, though sensitive types may not take kindly to unfamiliar riders. This system works both ways and reputable riding schools will not wish to accept badly schooled, traffic-shy or nappy animals on this basis.

WEEKDAY TIME COMMITMENT: Travelling and riding time only.

Full livery

The owner places his horse at a yard which accepts full responsibility for the feeding, mucking out, grooming, exercise and tack cleaning of the horse, leaving the owner with the choice of when to ride. On paper this is the most expensive way of keeping a horse but in fact when one considers the invisible costs incurred by part-DIY owners (as outlined earlier in this chapter), it can work out relatively inexpensively. The main area of difficulty tends to be over the interpretation of the word 'exercise'. Due to staff shortages, on days when the owner cannot ride, the exercise given may only comprise a 20-minute lungeing session or a quick hack round the block plus some time in the field. This is not enough to keep a horse fit for the sort of owner who wants to go on a 3-hour hack to get his money's worth at weekends, let alone for hunting or strenuous competition, and if the owner wants his horse to have a proper work-out he may find he has to pay a supplementary fee, which can inflate the weekly livery cost to £80-odd pounds a week. If your horse is well schooled you may find that it falls into the working livery category. If the yard tends to use your animal for staff lessons when they are being paid to exercise it and are clearly benefiting from such use of your animal, ask for a discount on the grounds that it is being treated like a working livery.

SUITABLE LIFESTYLES: Any – though it has to be said that those who can afford it are not in the target readership for this book.

SUITABLE HORSES: Any, but don't be disappointed if your horse fails to recognise you.

WEEKDAY TIME COMMITMENT: As working livery.

OTHER SYSTEMS

Communal yards

A logical, though relatively uncommon, development from sharing field rental with a friend is to club together with a dozen or so like-minded people and rent a whole yard which you run yourselves on a mutual-help basis.

This can be highly cost-effective for the working horse owner, as he can obtain stabling, storage space, grazing and maybe even a manège for half the price it would cost to rent those same facilities as an individual at the commercial yard. By sharing tasks the commune-members avoid labour charges, and each owner can go away on holiday or maybe even arrange one horse-free day a week without worry. Because the chances of everyone working exactly the same hours are fairly low, by staggering visits the owners can ensure that their horses have near round-the-clock attention – maybe even better than that supplied at a reputable full livery yard

– which compensates for the inevitable fact that none of you live on the spot. Further savings in time and money can be obtained by joining together to bulk buy hay, feed and bedding at a discount at favourable times of year, thus saving individuals time-consuming visits to the feed merchants. You could also consider joint purchase of time-saving gadgets like electric groomers or infra-red lamps – items which can make it so much easier for the clock-watcher to keep his horse in good condition yet which he could not entertain buying on his own.

There are problems, of course, as someone will have to act as overall manager, handle the books and liaise with the landlord. This is an enormous commitment for anyone who already has a full-time job and a house to run, and ideally the person who takes on this task should be compensated in some way. In my experience, however willingly someone takes on tasks at a yard of any kind, they soon become resentful if they think they are doing more than their share and this can soon develop into tensions which affect the smooth running of the enterprise. There are problems, too, if some of the commune members wish to leave and cannot immediately be replaced; the system suddenly becomes less economically attractive if others have to bear the cost of two or three empty box spaces over several months. And if you wish to leave the yard, it may not always be possible to reclaim the capital you have invested in equipment or, for example, the winter's supply of hay. In addition, the landlord may require a quarterly or annual rent in advance, which some may find less convenient than paying rental or livery on a weekly basis. It is as well to have a bolt-hole up your sleeve, too. Communal yards are only attractive because they represent a saving to the horse owner. If the landlord decides he can do better out of letting the yard to someone who wants to run it commercially at an increased rent, when the lease is up, you may find that it is no longer worthwhile continuing your group.

SUITABLE LIFESTYLES: As keeping a horse at home or at DIY livery.

SUITABLE HORSES: Any.

TIME COMMITMENT: As keeping a horse at home or on DIY livery, but with need for flexibility because of job-sharing requirement on certain days.

Barns and corrals

These two systems are commonly practised in Europe and the USA but are seen rather less in Britain. Circumstances are changing, however, and a lack of grazing in semi-rural and urban areas has meant that more people are having to use them. In both cases large numbers of horses are kept wholly or partly under cover in a relatively small area, usually no bigger than the standard 40 x 20 metre manège, and are fed communally on *ad lib* hay, with hard feed according to individual requirements. In areas where grazing is scarce, the fact that the horse has some kind of freedom gives this system a big plus over 24-hour stabling. I kept a three-year-old in this way with other youngsters during a severe winter and I have to say that he did very well on it. Even though he was at livery it cost me only a fraction more than having him out in a muddy, wet field. What little experience I have of the corral system for mature, working horses does lead me to suggest that it is less desirable for horses in relatively little work. As with the inadequately exercised stabled horse, corralled horses kept in a limited space and on a mainly dry diet will look for other distractions if they are not adequately exercised and, in the case of barning or corralling, this will inevitably mean picking fights with their companions. I have seen the corral system work brilliantly in Austria, where sixteen animals were kept together in a small dirt patch. But perhaps they settled down to eating for the night without fighting or bullying because they were trekking animals who did the best part of six hours' work a day!

SUITABLE LIFESTYLES: As grass livery, but the owner has a greater moral obligation to exercise the horse daily to help keep it sane in this relatively boring environment.

SUITABLE HORSES: Those in regular work; not suitable for resting or lightly worked animals as they are likely to suffer from boredom. Not suitable for timid animals or poor doers who are likely to lose out in the course of communal feeding.

WEEKDAY TIME COMMITMENT: As grass livery.

Tethering

At the time of writing, proposed legislation will make it illegal to *cruelly* tether an animal. Welfare organisations are lobbying to see

27

the practice completely wiped out. I cannot endorse or recommend the practice, for even with proper supervision tethering can go wrong, causing pain and distress if not an agonising death by strangulation. It has to be said that the true travelling folk, who have generations of horsemanship in their blood, operate the system successfully, but it has to be remembered that their lifestyle enables their horses to be under almost constant supervision – hardly the lot of the horse whose owner goes to work. It would also be irresponsible to avoid discussion of the system while tethering in any form remains legal. Certainly for many horses kept in urban areas tethering is the only way they can fulfil the instinct to move about and stretch their limbs and to pick at some grass. I also have to concede that my own, laminitis-prone cob is a lot happier if he is allowed to be tethered on a starvation patch for a few hours a day than to be holed up in his stable when the spring grass is at its richest without anything to eat or anywhere to stroll.

In view of this, those who feel they have no alternative are urged to obtain the Code of Practice for Tethering drawn up by the National Equine Welfare Committee and the RSPCA. A summary of it appears in the appendices at the back of this book.

SUITABLE LIFESTYLES: Few for the working owner, as he should have opportunity to break off from work and inspect horses several times a day.

SUITABLE HORSES: Only very quiet, non-blood type horses that are relatively unlikely to panic if they get entangled with the chain etc.

WEEKDAY TIME COMMITMENT: Ideally the horse should be checked two or three times a day, so there may be a lot of travelling just to service a cursory glance. Time involvement as grass livery.

Freelance help

In conjunction with some of the above systems, some working owners may find it cost-effective to employ independent part-time help. My own job in the magazine industry involves working one very late night on press day, in return for which I get the following morning off. Therefore I only really need help with my horses on four days a week, and in the past have often been irritated when charged by part-DIY livery yards for labour every day whether I need it or not.

In recent years there has been an increase in the number of people offering good value, flexible services as freelance grooms, usually working for three or four regular people for an hour or so each day, and acting as holiday relief. They can usually be found through cards on saddlery shop notice boards or through their advertisements in local papers, and of course by word of mouth. Personal recommendation is obviously desirable (one will be leaving a total stranger, possibly unsupervised, in charge of one's property as well as horses), as is reassurance about the person's ability in terms of recognised qualifications. However, anyone who is unreliable or inefficient does not usually last long in the freelance business, because each local equestrian community has a very fertile grapevine.

Generally, freelances bill clients once a week for their time, which can be flexible, plus travelling; the latter expense may not make the system viable for someone with just one horse. However, if you share the freelance with a friend who keeps his or her horse with or near yours, or if you have more than one horse, this method becomes much more attractive.

A few winters ago I was fortunate to have a particularly good girl Friday for my two stabled horses four days a week. In the mornings I would feed, ride, change rugs, turn out my horses and drain their soaked haynets before going to work. The freelance, having attended to her two other clients in the morning, would arrive at about 2 p.m. to do the mucking out, empty the barrows (plus my full skips from the night before), hang up the haynets and refill the water buckets. She would then catch up my two horses (who by this stage had been out for about six hours, more than enough for semi-clipped animals during the wettest and coldest part of the winter), wash off their legs, change their rugs and give them the mid-afternoon feed I had left prepared, putting the next day's hay in to soak before she left at around 3.30 p.m. I would then get home from work around 7 or 8 p.m. to give the horses their third feed of the day, brush them off, skip out, and top up their water and hay. The freelance did not come on my half day, when I did all the chores except, of course, bringing the horses in mid-afternoon. For just that one day a week I usually managed to persuade someone else to do the honours at no charge.

The beauty of this system is that your help comes in the form of a self-employed freelance, relieving you of all the obligations of the employer. It is entirely up to the freelance to pay her own insurance stamp or sort out a tax return. You also have no legal obligation to give a freelance notice when you no longer need his services, although it would be mean and immoral to drop someone without any warning when they had served you well. There are problems enough in the horse world without making any enemies.

There are, of course, disadvantages in using a freelance. These may include difficulty in contacting him or her with emergency messages when attending to other clients, problems if he falls sick, has transport difficulties or is delayed at a previous job, and the possibility that he could inadvertently bring disease into your yard from his other clients' horses. And, of course, he could easily let you down without notice. However, in my personal experience these eventualities are pretty remote and the advantages of using a freelance far outweigh the shortcomings, enabling you to have rather more say over the exact way your horses are treated at a cost comparable, if not even cheaper, to that offered for a rather less flexible service at a part- or DIY livery yard.

Horse sharing

The young person who already has a horse, or the person who finds he simply cannot cope with the time or financial commitment of having his own animal, may consider sharing the animal with another. This is only going to work to the advantage of both parties if working hours and lifestyles contrast so much that they both get value out of the animal by using it at different times. Unfortunately, in many cases both will want to ride at weekends, having limited time during the week. Therefore, although horse sharing may save individual's weekly costs, the horse will not necessarily be better managed and kept properly fit just because two people are caring for it.

The main choices are between literally going halves with someone over everything, from the purchase of the animal to its weekly running costs, or retaining ownership but allocating the third party so many days' use of the animal per week, in return for which he or she contributes to the running costs and does the stablework where appropriate. In the first case I most strongly recommend that you obtain legal advice to avoid the problems that can arise if you want to terminate the agreement – either to buy out your partner's half of the animal, or to get out of it altogether. I have seen several good friendships put under strain when there has been rivalry over a horse. Such arrangements are full of pitfalls and I have no intention of filling this space with advice that should come from someone with specialist qualifications.

The second choice at least offers the sole, legal owner the option to 'sack' the partner if the arrangement does not work, although again a written agreement is advisable.

A variation is to offer free riding on weekdays in return for some help. This might appeal, say, to a housewife who may have kept horses when younger but gave up when she married and started a family. It has the advantage of helping to keep your horse fit while saving money on labour. Great care should be taken when assessing a candidate as you must have faith in her sense of responsibility, as well as in her competence as a rider and handler. Ask yourself if you are being realistic to expect that someone 'paying' for riding, albeit in kind, will stick religiously to your exercising instructions; will they want to go for a 'burn-up' three times a week when your back is turned?

Although it may appeal – and you may well find eager takers – do not attempt to charge someone for the privilege of riding your horse while you are at work. As soon as you offer a horse 'for hire or reward', in the eyes of the law you become a riding establishment and will be subject to a host of unwanted rules and regulations.

Chapter 3

Choosing a livery yard

However much work the horse-owner is prepared to put in, if he is not able to keep his animal at home he is going to find that his enjoyment is very much dictated by his choice of livery yard or rented premises. Horse-keeping involves a lot of menial chores from which there is little respite. Whereas it is true that there are no genuine short-cuts in keeping a horse, many people are caused unnecessary extra work simply because their premises are badly laid out and ill-equipped. Some of the worst offenders are among the growing number of DIY livery yards which have sprung up in highly populated parts of the country, run by people who know there is money to be made simply by providing roofs over horses' heads. As a result the working owner can often find himself spending significant amounts of his so-called leisure time filling haynets in a dank, dark barn or shovelling manure into a wheelbarrow with a punctured tyre and having to struggle long distances across a mud patch to dump it.

Pedantic and petty as some of the time-saving suggestions in this chapter may seem, it is in the individual's own interests to carry out his own time and motion study and look for as many of them as possible when choosing a livery yard or indeed, when planning his own yard at home or elsewhere.

It can be very tempting to opt for the first place that boasts, for instance, an indoor school or miniature Badminton-type cross-country course, but if its general facilities are ill thought out, you could end up spending so much time on stable work that you do not have the time or energy to ride your horse round these luxuries except at weekends.

A more important reason for care when choosing a livery yard, however, is that, unlike commercial riding schools, livery yards are not covered by the compulsory local authority licensing schemes and relatively few take part in the voluntary approval schemes run by the BHS and the ABRS. Often commercial riding schools take liveries as a side-line, in which case you should be able to assume that one with BHS or ABRS approval will care for clients' horses as they would their own. However, many livery yards are run essentially as money-spinners by private individuals who take in 'paying guests' as a means of subsidising their own animals rather than as a proper business concern.

You will have to rely on gut-feelings and be prepared to ask awkward questions when assessing a yard. In the horse world first impressions are often, though not always, correct. If the yard is clean and well swept, the buildings, fences and gates well maintained, the staff tidily dressed and the horses blooming and interested in what is going on outside, you can be fairly confident that the stable management is meticulous across the board. This does not necessarily mean that yards that have not been swept on the day of your visit, or that have a muck-heap in total disarray, are undesirable; it may well be that the yard is run by busy people with other jobs, like yourself, and that they have got their priorities right in seeing to the horse's basic needs rather than fussing about appearances. However, I would recommend a first-time horse-keeper to look for bristling efficiency rather than a hope-for-the-best approach when selecting a yard, especially if it is to be supervising your animal 22 hours of the day.

Locations

If you have a good livery yard on your doorstep, run by people you like and in whom you feel confident, you are a member of a very lucky minority. Apart from the obvious advantages of being able to attend to your horse before and after work and again late at night, you are well placed to cope with emergencies; in the event of unexpected transport difficulties for instance, you can at least get there on foot.

Failing that, to minimise the amount of travel you should try to place your horse somewhere on a direct line between your home and your place of work. Having kept my two horses up to 10 miles from my home on a part-DIY basis for many years I would strongly recommend that if you can't find what you want near home then you should try to stable your horse as near to your workplace as possible. The extra long trip at weekends may prove irritating but the advantage of having the horse near your place of work five days a week will become evident in the winter when the precious daylight hours are on your side; even on the shortest day of the year, those without indoor or floodlit riding facilities should still be able to fit in a 20-minute lungeing session in near daylight and still be away from the yard by 8.45 a.m.

At present, as a rail commuter with a 90-mile round trip to my office in London, I have compromised on the above and have my horses 8 miles from home – but only ½ mile from a main line railway station. This works very well in the winter; I muck out, feed, water and prepare the evening feeds and haynets and ride one, if not two horses and then turn out in all but the worst weather before catching a train at 9 a.m. The horses are brought in for me late afternoon and when I get home at around 7 or 8 p.m. I go straight to the stables from the station.

Such relatively late visits enable the owner to top up water buckets and haynets, give a further feed where required and skip out (thus conserving bedding and saving time on the next morning's mucking out). The whole exercise takes only 20 minutes for two horses yet they appreciate the visit, seem to settle better for the night and, from the owner's point of view, they are out of the way before the evening's social and/or domestic commitments begin.

Of greatest importance, a regime like this also reduces the time the horses go without attention during the night. It is a regrettable fact that many DIY livery owners 'put their horses to bed' and are away from the yard by 5 p.m. The horses may not see them again until 8 or 9 a.m. the next day – maybe even later at weekends. Whereas it is perfectly acceptable to visit a horse at grass just once or twice a day, the stabled animal must have as near to round-the-clock attention as you can achieve to compensate for the boredom and lack of freedom dictated by his environment.

Riding facilities

If you have a full-time job your riding time on weekdays will be extremely limited. Of course, if you are prepared to get up at 5 a.m. every day – and many people are – in summer there is no reason why you shouldn't go for a two-hour hack every day before work. I do find, however, that after a start quite as early as this I get very tired by mid-afternoon and my work is certainly affected; the last thing you want to do is jeopardise the employment that pays for your hobby.

The facilities offered by the livery yard, and its surrounding countryside, should be carefully scrutinised before any firm decision is made to move the horse to it, so that you and your horse will reap the maximum benefit from your riding time. No horse should be expected to compete, hunt or do anything more strenuous than light hacking at weekends if he has not been worked during the week; even three or four ½-hour sessions midweek should be enough to keep the edge on an already fit horse that is expected to compete in dressage or show jumping at weekends.

In winter months especially, many DIY livery clients rely heavily on the opportunity to turn out stabled horses while they are at work during the day, and undoubtedly a mooch about the field helps to keep the horse's mind, wind and circulation right. However, this weekday exercise alone will not tone up the muscles he will use when being ridden.

If your proposed livery yard does not have an indoor school or an all-weather riding area for winter work, the next thing to consider is accessibility of good riding country. Ideally, you should be sur-rounded by a network of bridleways or other public open space, but I have often found that a variety of 40-minute routes round country lanes and even quiet residential areas have satisfactorily fulfilled my horses' exercise requirements when combined with turning out. It may appeal to move to a yard that is only a 15-minute hack from a beautiful park full of bridleways and long grassy canters when the long summer evenings are at your disposal, but on winter weekdays you won't have the time to get there and back, let alone to enjoy the open spaces. Aspiring competition riders should also check the nature of the riding country near by; it is a lot easier to put the foundations on your horse's fitness in a limited amount of riding time in undulating countryside with a variety of uphill pulls rather than flat commonland.

In addition, check whether you need permits or other authority to ride on adjacent ground, which is usually the case on Forestry Commission and Ministry of Defence land. Apart from the fact that permits can add significantly to your hidden costs, there is always the chance that they may not be immediately available. There is nothing worse than moving to a new area and applying for a pass only to discover that there is a waiting list and that you are therefore effectively grounded. People do, of course, ride out without author-ity and take their chance, but living in fear of being challenged by a warden does rather detract from one's enjoyment.

Use of the yard's own schooling facilities is often subject to additional fees, and unsuspecting livery clients could find that their first week's bill has doubled because they used the manège every day without having first checked out the terms of use. I once kept horses – briefly – at a centre whose jumping paddock was only available at an extra fee *and* only if one had a jumping lesson with the resident instructor, when I was already happy with the trainer I had elsewhere.

Indoor schools and manèges may also only be available to livery clients at certain times of day. Riding schools and private owners often require exclusive use of these facilities to get the training of their own animals out of the way before the day's business begins – exactly the same time that the working owner wants to ride. Equally, they may, quite rightly, try to recoup some of their enormous capital outlay by hiring out facilities to outsiders at all times of day and night. If you want to ride after dark you should expect to pay towards lighting, even if your use of the school is free at other times.

Stables and fields

Once you have established that the centre is located and/or equipped to offer the best use of your riding time, the next thing to consider is the suitability of the horse-keeping facilities. This, at first sight, will appear to be an odd set of priorities: surely the horse's well-being should come first? Certainly, if you plan to have your horse at full livery the level of care offered should be right at the top of your list. However, the DIY or part-DIY livery owner is directly responsible for his horse's exercise, feeding, bedding and cleanliness, and thus when assessing a yard you should be looking more at the 'back up' horse care provided in your absence. For the part-DIY, working owner, these requirements will most likely be turning out and bringing in of the horse, rugging up and presentation of feeds and haynets that you have in all probability left prepared.

A fair impression of the yard's attitude to horse care can often be gained from inspection of the gates and fencing in fields used by liveries. Alarm bells should ring in your head if access is through ill-fitting slip-rails or broken-down gates that are propped up against sagging posts and secured by binder twine. Apart from the fact that wrestling with such contraptions wastes valuable minutes for the clock-watching owner, it is also potentially hazardous; just try keeping control of one horse with one hand while trying to shift a heavy gate and deterring a third party from escaping with the other – and often in deep mud too!

A situation to be avoided; ill-fitting gates are difficult to open, waste time and also distract the handler from the horse.

In the course of my work as an equestrian journalist I have had the chance to visit the yards of one or two distinguished equestrian personalities whose amenities have, on paper, left much to be desired, yet who produce happy, healthy and successful horses despite an apparently great potential for accidents at home. Gates and fences do indeed represent an enormous expense and undeniably there are numerous caring yards that genuinely cannot afford to keep them in perfect condition. But poor maintenance of these items can also indicate general sloppiness and inefficiency in the running of the whole establishment and is something that working owners who cannot give their horses 24-hour supervision should bear in mind.

Ideally there should be a number of small paddocks or 'play pens' into which stabled horses can be turned out for at least three hours a day, either singly or with a proven friend. Again, alarm bells should ring if the yard appears to have only one field, albeit a large one. This almost certainly means that your horse will either only be able to go out for an hour or so, so that all those needing to be turned out can be fitted in during the working day, or that all the horses go out together and he will just have to 'muck in' with the gang. Certainly, one of the greatest problems the livery yard owner

37

faces is pleasing all of his clients all of the time over turn-out; no one wants his horse to be kicked or otherwise injured by a strange horse while his back is turned, although it does not follow that this is more likely to happen if there are half a dozen animals in the field instead of one or two. Provided proper care is taken in introducing new animals to the 'herd', a pecking order will soon be established between the horses and yours will soon know how to avoid trouble. If, however, the yard persists in grazing an habitual bully with the rest of the liveries despite complaints from other clients there is not, frankly, a lot that can be done. DIY owners beset with this problem should consider moving elsewhere; there is no pleasure in sitting at work worrying all day about whether or not you will find an injured horse when you return to the yard at night.

Problems over turn-out are more likely to occur if the field used for horses stabled at night is also the permanent abode of the grass liveries who live out all or part of the year round.

Trying to extract your horse from a group of ponies milling round the gate at tea-time can be a fraught experience. Likewise, you will also incur the justifiable wrath of their owners if you frequently arrive late to bring in your own horse during the dark winter nights when they are waiting to put out hay and feed.

There are two other considerations for the DIY owner regarding yards with limited turn-out facilities. First, if there is only one field, does the yard make alternative grazing arrangements in the winter, or will it impose a blanket ban on grazing and oblige clients to stable their horses full-time to save the land? Second, if the fields are so busy that they are never rested, how good and how plentiful will the grazing be, and will it be infested with worms? If you have no choice other than to keep a horse on such over-grazed land you should consult your veterinary surgeon about the possible need for a more frequent than usual worming programme and supplementary feeding if your horse's health is not to suffer, and this of course will add to your costs.

The fields available to liveries living out all year round, or turned out during the day in all weathers, should have an open-fronted shelter to accommodate the numbers that may wish to use it at any one time, either to get out of wind and driving rain in the winter or to escape from flies and heat in the summer months. Failing that, a line of stout hedging, trees or other natural wind-breaks should be available to provide shelter – and indeed horses often prefer them to the man-made variety. In the absence of any of these, ask the proprietor if staff will bring your horse in for you earlier than usual in adverse conditions – and if so, is there an extra charge for this service.

From the point of view of security and for saving time, gates to fields should be as near as possible to the stable yard and not open directly on to the road or other public right of way.

As far as the stabling itself is concerned, never fall into the trap of rejecting a yard just because it does not conform to the stereotype quadrangle with flower-baskets and a weathervane on the roof. Many people have made some ingenious conversions from unlikely premises (some friends of mine transformed a disused brickworks into a super yard). The DIY owner's priority should be the comfort and safety of the accommodation offered to the horse that is not being supervised full-time, not what it looks like from the outside, and how the stable allocated is situated in relation to the feed shed, barn, tack room and muck heap.

Horses are very gregarious by nature and although many people successfully keep single horses without companionship, they tend to fret if they cannot see another horse. Certainly stabled horses kept on their own need a lot of entertainment – regular and varied exercise, food split up into four or five lots a day and a good strapping session at night – if they are to be kept happy in the absence of their own kind, which is something the working owner has little hope of offering. Sometimes private establishments that take in the odd livery will place your horse away from the main stable block so that your unconventional hours do not interfere with the running of the main establishment. There is a lot of sense in this, as anyone who has seen the disturbance that can be caused when only one horse in a block gets a feed will agree. But it can be miserable for the poor animal who goes for hours on end with nothing to see – and worse still, no one to see him if he gets cast or is taken ill in his owner's absence. It is completely against the horse's nature to be isolated in a confined space. Bored horses quickly develop vices such as weaving (when the horse rocks on his legs from side to side) or wind-sucking (when the horse grasps the top of the stable door, manger or any other handy projection simultaneously gulping in air). These habits are almost impossible to break; both can damage the horse's health; and from a purely selfish point of view, they devalue the animal. Some yards will refuse to admit horses with these vices unless they continue to be kept in isolation, and with justification. Horses, bored or not, are highly susceptible to the habits of others.

The American barn – facing rows of stables indoors or with

the aisle under some sort of cover – is catching on in Britain and has a lot to recommend it for the DIY owner, not least the opportunity to avoid getting wet in bad weather when carrying out stable chores before hurrying off to work. The atmosphere in a closed environment can be dusty, however, and if your horse is one of the many that seem to have allergies and related respiratory problems this environment could cause you extra problems – and extra work.

If your horse has a mild cough which has to be managed by soaking hay and bedding him on shavings, paper or other dust-free materials, you should in any case ask for a stable next to other horses that are managed in a similar fashion. Fungal spores from 'dry' hay or straw in an adjacent box will invariably set off a cough in your own horse, however clean you keep your own stable.

The stable offered should be as large, roomy and airy as possible without draughts. A box in which a horse is going to spend 22 hours of the day should be at least 12 x 12 ft (3.6 x 3.6 m) although 12 x 10 ft (3.6 x 3 m) may be acceptable for an animal of up to 16 hh that is out in the field for the best part of the day. It does not matter whether it is brick or timber, although it has to be said that the former is usually warmer in winter and cooler in summer, and that owners of horses inclined to chew should try to avoid the latter unless they are prepared to reinstate or pay for any damage done to the interior of the box. Roofing materials vary considerably; corrugated iron is undesirable because it is cold in winter. Felt and board is popular and inexpensive on timber boxes but usually needs overhauling and replacing when two or three years old, which is something the client should check; a modern alternative is a corrugated type of plastic, which is extremely durable but tends to encourage excessive condensation in the winter – I have known rugs to get soaked on horses stabled under this roofing.

The stable should be free of broken fittings, split wood panelling or other projections on which the horse could injure himself, and have a bottom door which opens freely and is not handicapped by bolts that stick and have to be wrenched open. A box with such shortcomings should not be rejected if the yard suits you in other respects. In my experience proprietors rarely complain if you want to do your own running repairs to their buildings and it is not unduly difficult or expensive to repair or replace fittings that will make the box safer and easier to manage.

Making *structural* alterations to other peoples' property is, however, quite a different matter, for which reason I would be wary of accepting a timber box of an economy brand, the type offered to DIY liveries in many newly set up yards. The quality of timber and durability of the some 'budget line' boxes is not necessarily inferior – I have had some myself and have been extremely pleased with them. But in many cases the manufacturers have kept the price down by providing a lower pitched roof than that of the 'luxury' brands, with a fixed window rather than one that opens. The resulting lack of cubic airspace and restricted ventilation means that these boxes tend to heat up very quickly during the summer months and this can be hell for the horse stabled during the day. It can be quite a shock for the owner to arrive at the stables in the evening and find a horse dripping with sweat simply as a result of standing in. Worse still, the working owner who is only able to visit his stabled horse early in the morning and late at night when the temperature has dropped could go several days without being aware of the cause of the problem. Likewise, if there is a lack of ventilation you cannot safely shut the top stable door in severe winter weather. If you have such a stable of your own you can probably persuade a handyman in the family to alter the window so that it opens, insert a slip rail attachment so that the bottom door can be flung wide in hot weather, and take a plank or two out of the top of the back wall to encourage the airflow. If you are offered such a box, there is no harm in asking the owner if he would agree to alterations.

The stable floor should be inspected carefully. Traditionally stable floors are made of brick or, less ideally, concrete, the surface of which has been roughened with a herringbone-type pattern to assist drainage and more importantly to make the surface non-slip. Some floors may simply be compacted earth or chalk, which when damp can be extremely slippery for horse and owner and should be avoided; I have lost my footing several times on the latter – not funny when you have a pitchfork in your hand.

The floor itself should have a gentle slope towards the front to further assist drainage. Regrettably, in yards hastily constructed expressly for DIY livery clients, this requirement is sometimes overlooked and you should bear in mind that a level stable floor, or one with depressions where moisture can gather, is going to be just that bit more difficult and therefore time-consuming to keep clean. One solution, if you feel you can justify the cost, may be to invest in temporary stable flooring. One of the new ones on the market is a kind of perforated non-slip matting which you buy to your requirements, as you would carpet squares. It allows urine to pass through and therefore gives your bedding a longer life as

41

well as saving time on mucking out. The other main advantage is, of course, that you can take it with you when you go, and it is therefore obviously preferable to making any structural alterations to the floor of a box you do not own. Beware, however, of trying to compromise by using other types of slotted rubber matting, especially that which is reinforced with metal and liable to split – an obvious safety hazard.

The stable should be as near as possible to the feed room, hay barn, tack room and muck-heap for the obvious reason of saving time. Even a minute saved on all these trips is crucial for the clock-watcher.

Taps should ideally be outside along the wall of the stable block at intervals of three or four boxes, rather than there being a sole water outlet a good hike away. If you are lucky the boxes may be equipped with automatic-filling drinking bowls, but these are only desirable if they incorporate a gauge which shows how much the horse is drinking. You will also have to clean out the bowl every few days, as bits of food will drop into it from the horse's mouth, tainting the water and maybe clogging up the mechanism; on balance if may be as quick to stick to buckets.

Automatic feeding machines are a boon for the DIY owner who wants his horse to have breakfast before he arrives to ride, or an extra feed at any time of day when no one is around to see to it personally. The units are situated over a corner manger and some can be programmed to release eight or more small feeds in a 24-hour period. This adheres to the principle of feeding little and often more faithfully than the normal stable feeding routine and also offers the advantage of off-setting boredom for the horse stabled full-time. These units are rarely supplied by livery yards but proprietors are unlikely to object to you installing your own, especially if the timers are battery operated and won't affect the yard's electricity bill.

In some modern, 'high tech' stables there are hatches on the front wall through which feed can be poured into the manger, without the feeder having to go into the stable. These may look impressive but are of no real advantage to the DIY owner, whose regime dictates that he will nearly always feed when going into the box to complete one or more other stable tasks.

At most DIY yards you should expect to pay rental for the stable, use of facilities and the cost of labour for the tasks you cannot do yourself. However, the cost of feeding will vary. Some yards like to charge an all-inclusive fee for hard feed, hay and bedding, although this rarely works to the advantage of both parties; it can create ill-feeling if the horse is a particularly 'good doer' and the owner thinks he is paying for more food than he needs; likewise, the proprietor will become irritated if he thinks the client is helping himself to more shavings than he is entitled to. The ideal situation is for the proprietor to provide each client with ample storage space for three or four bales of hay, bedding and a couple of feed bins, and for the client to buy exactly what he needs when he wants it from the yard's main feed store. You may pay a few pence more than at the local feed merchant but in turn you will save time and car fuel. Using the hatchback to pick up a sack of nuts or the odd bale of shavings is a sure way of messing up – and devaluing – your car.

You should also not feel awkward about padlocking your feed bins (a dustbin can be secured by passing a length of chain through the handles on the sides and the lid) if you have to share storage with others. It is extraordinary how many normally upright citizens will not think twice about helping themselves to someone else's feed if they are about to run out, and yet fail to replace the scoop of nuts they have borrowed when they get their new feed supply. Even if this happens only once a fortnight you could end up losing £10 worth of feed a year. I was once at a yard where a fellow livery owner managed to feed her horse free for two months by helping herself to the contents of the bins of the dozen other clients until she was caught topping up her own bins when someone made an unscheduled late night visit to the yard.

Company

No one who keeps horses needs to be told that it is not just a hobby, it is a way of life. The person who keeps his horse at livery is going to be spending three hours or more in the company of the same bunch of people every day, so it may be prudent to find out the age range of the yard's other clients before you make a firm decision to go there. Although it happens a lot, it surely cannot be healthy for a school-leaver to spend a significant amount of her social life with a group of women her mother's age, or for a young professional woman to be in a yard with the proverbial party of screaming kids! If you are working hard to earn enough money to keep a horse that you only have limited time to ride, you owe it to yourself to make sure every aspect of it provides fun.

43

Terms and conditions

It is extremely important to clarify terms and conditions before making a decision about moving to a new yard. Proprietor and client should be under no misunderstanding about how responsibility for the horse's welfare is to be shared. There is nothing worse than being delayed at work and returning to the yard at 8 p.m. on a wet winter's night to find your animal shivering by the gate because the yard thought you had intended to bring him in yourself that day. Ask the yard to outline the services they will do regularly and how much it will cost, and how much you pay for occasional extra help if you are unexpectedly absent. Most people will be wanting to keep labour costs as low as possible by doing the bulk of the stable chores themselves. But beware of over-committing yourself; most proprietors expect to stand in for you in emergencies but their goodwill should not be taken for granted if you have to work late or want to make last-minute social arrangements which prevent you fulfilling, say, your evening stables' commitment on a regular basis. Even if you are willing to pay, it does not necessarily mean that a staff member is available to do the extra work. Such attitudes do not foster good client-proprietor relationships.

If you move to a yard during the winter and keep your horse in, and then opt to have it out at grass during the summer to save money, do not assume that a box will automatically be available for you the following winter – ask. No commercial yard can afford to have boxes standing idle and it is possible that during the summer 'your' stable gets a new, full-time occupant. Surprisingly, in my experience livery yards rarely ask for a retention fee from owners who want to reserve a box for the winter, although they would be justified in so doing.

Instead of writing out a long list of questions covering every eventuality, it should be enough to ask if there are any hidden extras or any special or unusual terms you have missed in your discussions. For instance, the yard may advise you not to worry about shoeing – a farrier visits the yard on a regular basis and will take on your horse. But the manager may not quickly volunteer the information that if you can't be present, you will be charged for the time a staff member holds your horse while it is being shod. The same might well apply to veterinary visits.

You should also confirm how the yard will act in emergencies. Staff must have your office/work 'phone number as well as your home details, and must have permission to contact the vet direct if you cannot be traced immediately, plus instructions to notify your insurance company if you are away on holiday or business; the latter is very important as procedural technicalities can jeopardise the successful processing of a claim.

All parties should be clear about liability. Proprietors may ask you to sign a disclaimer which acquits them of any responsibility in the event of an accident or damage to your horse or property. This is a 'grey' area; if you are simply renting premises then it could be argued that safety and welfare of the horse is up to you but if you are paying for any kind of *service*, i.e. livery, the proprietors cannot contract out of negligence. Having said that, proving such negligence in the courts can be an expensive and stressful experience so it is best have your horse comprehensively insured. Then, in the event of a substantial claim, it is up to the insurance company to settle with you and sue the yard proprietor themselves if they feel your horse's claim resulted from some misdemeanour on their part.

Further discussion of the important subject of horse insurance is given later.

Chapter 4

Feeding

Knowing how and what to feed a horse is almost an art form. Ground rules have been developed over generations – a curious mixture of tradition and the results of scientific study – but at the end of the day the old saying 'the eye of the master maketh the horse fat' still sums it all up.

The working owner responsible for feeding his own horse faces particular problems as he clearly cannot keep breaking away from what he is doing to pop a feed into the stabled animal. Furthermore, if he keeps his horse at DIY livery or in communal yards, choice of feedstuffs and storage space may be limited.

For the novice, it can be difficult to assess the quantities the horse really needs. As a rough guide, the horse needs a total daily intake of about 2.5 lbs (1.1 kg) per 100 lbs (450 kg) of his bodyweight, which for a 16 hh horse would work out at 30 lbs (13 kg) of food a day. The difficulty is working out how the total volume should be split between bulk foods – hay and grass – and concentrates, the higher protein, 'hard' feeds like oats, barley or specially formulated nuts and cubes. Many good books contain specimen feed charts that appear to cover most types and circumstances but these can inadvertently mislead the novice because two animals of similar breeding, temperament and in identical work can have widely varying food conversion rates. By way of example I will mention just two of many cases known to me that went completely against the 'rule book'. One is my own 16 hh Thoroughbred, who, as a five- and six-year-old was being produced to BHS event by an experienced competitor. According to convention he should have been on 12-15 lbs (5.4-6.8 kg) concentrates a day – but we found he was popping out of his skin on 7 or 8 lbs (3-3.5 kg)! Another Thoroughbred living out in the summer with mine on good grazing should have been able to undertake the light hacking asked of him and keep his figure with a hard feed of 3 or 4 lbs (1.3-1.8 kg) a day. Yet his owner had to give him that much three times a day just to keep weight over his ribs. Obviously there is something fundamentally wrong with this horse's metabolism, but he serves to prove the point that each horse must be treated as an individual.

If you are horse-keeping for the first time, the obvious thing to do is to ask the previous owner for a detailed chart of quantities, your horse's likes and dislikes, and amend it accordingly if you are going to put him to significantly more or less work. One advantage of keeping a horse at livery is that there is likely to be someone around who can offer sound advice. If you are keeping the horse at home, or in rented premises on your own and have no knowledgeable person to call on, the lesser of the evils is to start off the part-stabled, part-grazed horse on unlimited bulk (i.e. hay or grass). On the assumption that initially the 16 hh part-bred is being ridden an hour a day, split 5 or 6 lbs (2.2-2.7 kg) of non-heating concentrates (i.e. nuts, not oats) into two feeds a day. Keep a careful eye on his weight and if he starts to look a fraction lean or fat you can amend the daily quantity by 1 or 2 lbs (0.45-0.9 kg) over the course of the week, and re-assess again. I must stress that I am *not* advocating deliberate under-feeding as a general rule. But on balance it is preferable to under-feed concentrates rather than over-feed in the short-term, for otherwise the working owner will end up with a horse too hot to handle in the limited time available, or possibly so overweight that he becomes ill. (Although the disease is commonly associated with spring grass, you can also bring on laminitis by over-feeding rich concentrates.)

It is generally much easier to put weight on a horse than to take it off when limited riding time is available. A horse should never be allowed to get too fat, especially when young. Excess weight puts extra strain on organs like the heart and lungs and can sometimes irreparably damage the joints which, in an animal whose usefulness depends on his locomotive ability, should always be treated with respect.

On the other hand, novice owners should be aware that a new horse can mislead them about his energy requirements in the first two weeks or so. With a new rider, and stimulating new sights and sounds, any horse will be lively to ride out until he settles down to his new home. High jinks in the first few days are not necessarily a sign that oats have gone to his head. Flexibility and commonsense must therefore go hand in hand with understanding and observation of the ground rules of feeding.

47

The rules of good feeding

• Feed little and often, as mentioned in the early chapters, so that the horse's natural method of eating round the clock is observed as far as possible. There are practical problems for the working owner, but when deciding how few feeds you can get away with giving daily, remember that the part-bred horse of 16 hh cannot efficiently digest more than 4-5 lbs (1.8-2.2 kg) of concentrates every four hours.

• Feed plenty of bulk – i.e. hay or grass – again to imitate the natural method and to assist the digestive system to work efficiently. This also applies to the concentrate ration. Whether comprised of traditional grains like oats or barley, or compounded nuts and mixes, 'hard' feed should contain bulk like chaff or bran to encourage mastication and therefore assist the digestive system.

• Stick to the same feeding hours. Horses thrive on routine. It does not matter if he gets breakfast at 9 a.m., lunch at 3.30 p.m. and tea at 7 p.m. *as long as these times are the same every day*.

• Water before feeding. If the horse is allowed to take a long drink after consuming a full feed, undigested food will be washed through the stomach and cause problems for the next digestive process, possibly leading to colic. A horse that has constant access to water is at less risk as he will frequently take a short drink during or after a feed. However, if he seems intent on swilling down the whole bucket on top of his feed I would recommend whipping it away for an hour or so before too much damage is done. Working owners need to pay particular attention to watering. When time is short on weekdays there is always a temptation to feed a horse immediately on return from exercise when he may still be hot and therefore even more likely to want a long drink after he has eaten.

• Feed according to work. Hard feeding needs to be so flexible that quantities are increased or reduced on an almost daily basis if the exercise routine changes. Hard feed should be increased if work increases but cut down or even right out if the horse is suddenly thrown out of work. This is because his body is not equipped to store carbohydrates in quantity and an accumulation of glycogen in resting muscles can trigger off a chain of metabolic problems which result in acute cramp-like symptoms, commonly known as 'tying up' or, somewhat inaccurately, azoturia, when the horse resumed strenuous work. When hard feed is cut, increase bulk to compensate.

• Do not ask a horse to carry out fast work on a stomach full of bulk – hay or grass – or after a full feed. There are two reasons for this, as previously described. First, because the blood supply will be diverted to fuelling the muscles and will detract from the efficiency of the digestive system; and second because the stomach is situated next to the lungs and, if full, will press on the chest and affect breathing. It takes a horse about 15-20 minutes to eat a full feed and 1½ hours to digest it. Observation of this rule will therefore determine the working owner's daily timetable – for instance, you may have to delay the horse's breakfast until after you have ridden, or get someone else to bring him in mid-afternoon from a field of good grass if you want to ride after you've finished work.

• Make no sudden changes in the diet. If you want to introduce a new type of corn, mineral supplement, or to drastically change the diet from, say, mixed corn to complete nuts, do so gradually, over a period of three to four days.

• Feed something succulent, again to imitate nature, especially if the horse does not have a daily spell at grass and is fully stabled on dry food rations. This might include carrots and apples, sugar-beet or grassmeal. In any event, dampen the concentrate ration with water to reduce dust and the risk of choking.

• Do not mix supplements or pre-mixed feedstuffs without reference to manufacturer's feeding instructions, or without veterinary advice. Most supplements, except those specifically formulated to cope with a particular deficiency, are balanced in themselves, but haphazard mixing could lead to unwitting dietary imbalances.

Storing feedstuffs

A common problem for the working owner who keeps his horse at premises away from home is storage of feed. One's choice will not depend solely on personal preference, as is the luxury of the full-time horse-keeper, but on suitability of storage and the facility to prepare specialist feeds correctly, especially if they are to be fed in your absence by someone else. A further irritation is that storage limitations will also prevent you from taking advantage of bulk buying at a discount. You may well have to resign yourself to missing out on hay bargains and paying over the odds for three or four bales at a time, wasting time fetching them in a trailer at weekends or, worse still, in the back of your car.

But lack of storage for bulk is not entirely disadvantageous where hard feed is concerned. The owner of only one or two horses should not attempt to store several months' worth of hard feed as, even if unopened, it will deteriorate and lose nutritional value over a month or so and maybe even get so stale that the horse refuses to eat it.

It is therefore useful to be able to buy your hard feed direct from your livery yard owner, even if slightly at a premium. First, you will save transporting time and costs, and second you should be able to assume that your sack is fresh because a busy yard should be getting a new feed delivery at least once a fortnight.

The facilities livery owners are given to store their feedstuffs may vary from lockable outbuildings containing galvanised bins to a precariously erected tarpaulin at the side of a shed. In any event, steps should be taken to keep the feed dry and away from vermin. Hay should be stored off the ground, ideally on wooden pallets or similar, to encourage airflow and keep off the moisture that will make it go mouldy. One-horse owners usually find it convenient to keep their individual feed supplies in dustbins, which are somewhat cheaper than traditional steel bins, a more useful size for the small quantities in use and easier to transport if and when you move yards. If the plastic variety is used the bins should be kept off the ground – I have known rats chew an enormous hole to get at the contents overnight. On grounds of economy and hygiene, keep the hard feedstuffs in the bag within the bin – do not pour them out. This prevents a build-up of stale crumbs at the bottom of the container.

Hay

When horse-keepers are obliged to buy hay direct from the premises where they graze or stable their animals, quality can be somewhat harder to control.

In the past, when choosing hay to buy in bulk horsemen would look for several different types – meadow, mixture, clover or sainfoin to name but a few – but today a lot of people have to accept what they can get. Because of the demand for bulk feedstuffs, especially in semi-suburban areas where horse-sick pasture means that hay has to be fed even to animals living out in the summer, many will cut hay from any sort of grazing. I have several friends who cut hay from grass they know to be inferior and sell it cheaply to a ready market, buying in better-quality forage for their own animals!

Buying cheap hay when you have the choice of better quality is false economy; if hay is of low feed value then the hard feed must be balanced to supply the nutrients that in the past one could have assumed were present in good hay.

Sometimes, too, hay may be too new. Meadow hay used to be thought ready for consumption when it had been in the stack for eighteen months – i.e. harvested in summer 1988 for use in the winter of 1989-90 – but often by necessity new hay that is less than six months old will be fed, although there is the danger that it may be indigestible.

The colour of hay will vary according to the type of grass it is cut from – but excess yellow or dark brown suggests deterioration due to overheating in the rick. Good hay will smell sweet and appetising, never musty or smoky. It should be crisp to the touch, and the sections of the bale should spring apart when the twine is cut. If instead the fibres stick together in compressed slabs, or reveal patches of mould and dust, the hay is quite unfit for feeding. First, this is because it may cause digestive disorders. Second, it offers nothing in the way of feed value. And thirdly, in all probability the horse, by nature a fastidious eater, will reject it and tread it into his bed, giving the owner-groom the dual headache of ensuring his horse consumes the essential bulk as well as extra work clearing the spurned food from the bedding.

Sales of goods legislation is, in theory, on your side; hay, like anything else that is sold, should be of 'merchantable quality'. If on opening a bale you find it inferior you are entitled to ask for a replacement. In practice, however, owners are inclined to put up with it, slinging out the bad bits and making do with the edible sections, rather than risking any unpleasantness with the yard owner. But if this problem persists you may have to get in your own hay from elsewhere, however inconvenient, or try one of the hay substitutes mentioned below.

Sometimes hay that smells sweet and is apparently mould-free will nonetheless be dusty. Again, if this is all you can get I would strongly recommend soaking it in a bin or trough of water for 12-24 hours (i.e. overnight) to counteract the harmful effect of spores that can cause respiratory disorders. Mindful of the potential for problems with modern-day hay, several well-known competition riders soak *all* the hay fed to their animals, whether they have existing wind problems or not.

The lone owner-groom will generally find it most convenient to put the required amount of hay in a net and soak it in a small dustbin, but in big yards, whole bales may be done at a time in a disused bath, trough, or cistern liner, owners helping themselves as required. A problem with the latter procedure is that there can be a tendency to keep using the same tainted water, albeit topped up, and for stale, slimy pieces of hay to get mixed up with the new, making the wet hay less palatable and maybe even harmful. The water should be completely changed every 24 hours.

A soaked haynet holds an incredible amount of water and will need to be drained for at least threequarters of an hour before it is offered to the horse. You must therefore remember to remove it from the bin as soon as you arrive at the yard in the morning so that it is ready to be hung in the stable before you leave for work, unless you have someone to do it for you. If not, it will be very heavy, tempting you to drag it along the ground, and it will drain into the bedding. A useful tip is to soak hay in a hessian sack, which prevents bits of hay falling out over the yard between trough and stable and may save you some valuable sweeping-up time. Some people like to feed hay in small quantities to further reduce waste; certainly a lot of wet hay can be trampled into the bed and therefore rendered inedible. However, to do this you need three haynets on the go at once – one in soak, one hanging up to drain and one being fed – which may not fit in with a regime based on two yard visits a day.

An alternative to soaking hay is steaming; you put the haynet in a stout, leak-free plastic bag and pour over one or two kettles of boiling water, then seal the top and leave it to steam for an hour or two. Many vets say it is not as efficient as soaking for allaying the effects of fungal spores, though it is a useful stop-gap if you have forgotten or run out of time to soak the hay overnight. Steaming has the bonus of making hay smell more appetising and can tempt the sick or off-colour horse (though it should *not* be viewed as a means of trying to persuade a fit horse to eat inferior hay!), but it can also make the droppings rather loose if fed on several consecutive days.

The quickest way to feed hay is off the floor, but few horses keep the pile tidy and much of the hay will be dragged into the bed and wasted. The filling of haynets is time-consuming but feeding hay this way is the most economical; if you prepare them for other people to tie up in your absence it is also ensures the horse gets exactly the quantities you require. Working owners will have to discipline themselves to prepare haynets the night before, when more time is available. This also gives the owner the opportunity to shake out the hay and check for foreign bodies – a safety precaution frequently overlooked in the morning by those who find it quicker to fill nets by the two or three section-load.

In some older stables eye-level hay-racks are provided. In theory these are ideal as they are quickly filled, but in practice their use should be avoided. First, the horse has to adopt an unnatural stance for several hours to eat the hay; and second, seeds and other small bits will drop down and can set up irritations in the eye. The modern equivalent, surprisingly not extensively used, is the solid-sided, low-level variety which enables the horse to eat the hay from a lower, chest height and is also quicker to fill; if you have a good drain the rack can be situated on that side of the box and therefore wet hay can be put in straight out of the soaking bin. They can be bought or home-made but the accent is on the solid-sided; if the racks are slatted like the eye-level variety the horse could get his foot caught in them.

A modern method of ensiling fresh grass has resulted in several brands of 'hages' and 'lages' making their mark as equine feedstuffs. The process of vacuum-packing cut grass straight off the field has produced a bulk feed offering a higher protein content than hay and, more importantly, one that is completely dust-free. It is now widely fed in competition and training yards to offset respiratory disorders. It is more expensive than hay but

A solid-sided chest- or ground-level hay-rack which is quick to fill and also encourages the horse to eat from a more natural angle than the haynet or traditional eye-level hay-rack.

the producers argue that users save on the hard feed bill because of the superior nutritive quality of the 'hage'.

'Hage' obviously offers great advantages to the busy owner; it has a consistently high level of quality which solves the problem of having to buy poor hay from your landlord; it relieves the owner of a horse with a 'wind' problem of the time-consuming chore of soaking; and as bales come packed in sealed polythene bags they are also easier to collect in the car in small numbers at a time. However, as a working owner I have not found 'hages' ideal for the animal that is stabled most of the time. First, this is because 'hages' tend to be so rich that only a small volume is fed compared with hay; as a result the horse eats it very quickly and thus the 'entertainment' value of the bulk feed is lost on the horse that spends many hours alone while his owner is at work. (You can buy special 'hage'-nets with a tight mesh that slows down the eating process but in the case of my own admittedly greedy animals this has not made a significant difference to the eating time.) Second, 'hage' has to be carefully stored and quickly used once opened. If the bags are unwittingly pierced and air gets in, the contents can be spoiled; 'hage' found to be contaminated or mouldy on opening should not be fed on any account. Storage for livery owners can be a problem, and if you have to use a communal shed, put your 'hage' out of the way where it cannot inadvertently be pricked by stable forks and or other such items carelessly tossed aside by other rushing riders.

In recent years the development of hydroponic grass-growing machines has meant that the fully stabled horse can be fed a sizeable succulent ration all year round – a boon for those in urban environments where grazing is not available. As these machines are expensive they cannot merit detailed discussion in a book aimed at one-horse owner-riders. If you are lucky enough to be in a yard that has one, check the suitability of the grass for your own animal before accepting it; different types of seed are available which range in nutritive value.

Hard feed

Concentrates or 'hard' feed in common use are discussed below. Basic grains like oats, barley and bran still form the staple diet in many yards, despite the great advances being made in pre-formulated mixes and compound feeds. But I would like to shirk convention and start by making a case for the feeding of 'nuts' or complete feeds by working owners or the inexperienced, and for

54

those who have limited storage or little control over the quality of basic oats, barley, etc. supplied by the premises where they keep their horse.

First, formulated nuts or cereal mixes prepared by a reputable brand name offer a consistent level of quality and nutritional balance, which you can only guess at in the case of basic grains that could have come from a variety of different mills. A lot of owners like to mix their own feeds, taking the view that they like to *see* exactly what they are feeding their horse. Frankly, they are deluding themselves as two identical-looking samples of oats could have a digestible protein content as variable as 6 and 16 per cent. I don't think that any horse-keeper could claim that he has the time or money to get every sack of feed laboratory analysed. At least most well-known brand names state the nutritive content on the sack.

Second, complete feeds save the owner considerable time in preparation, not only in terms of having to measure out scoopfuls from three or four sacks. The methods by which most complete feedstuffs are prepared make them more digestible; however, optimum digestibility of some traditional feedstuffs like oats and barley can often be achieved by boiling, a further time-consuming chore and also an inconvenience for the owner who does not have cooking facilities where he keeps his horse.

Third, you only need to have one sack of 'complete' feed opened at once, which should mean that you get through it before it starts to go off. A one-horse owner with several sacks of oats, maize, bran and barley on the go at once may take a month to use up the supply and, during the summer especially, such corn can easily get stale and 'clammy'.

Fourth, complete or pre-mixed feeds simplify feeding and reduce the scope for error if you ask other people in a busy yard to feed your horse when you are at work.

Fifth, cubes are usually dust-free, while pre-mixed cereals are frequently dampened down by molasses, which also has a preservative effect. This means that they are more suitable for use in automatic feeding units as there is no sticky matter to clog up the works.

On the minus side, complete feeds cost more *pro rata* than basic grains and sometimes you may be paying for a higher protein content than you need. Certainly the ordinary riding horse does not want any grain with a protein content of more than 9 per cent. The protein content should be stated on the side of the feed sack. If it is not, any cereal mix which on inspection appears to contain a noticeable amount of beans – soya or locust bean – should be fed with caution as these are two very high-protein, heating foods which can literally blow the minds of most ordinary riding horses. One should also distinguish between completely balanced compound feeds and specially formulated feeds like Bailey's meal, which is more generally fed in conjunction with traditional grains.

Another problem is that pre-mixed feeds and nuts tend to be more dense and could cause those who measure everything by the scoopful instead of weighing it to inadvertently over-feed.

Lastly, complete feeds only contribute to a balanced diet if they are fed according to the manufacturer's instructions, if they form a significant proportion of the daily food intake and are not haphazardly mixed with other grains. If your horse is a good doer and seems to thrive on hay or grass in the summer months, a mere token feed of nuts is obviously not going to supply his daily mineral and vitamin needs. In this case it would be more effective to pop a daily recommended dose of a proprietary supplement, bought in powder or liquid form, in a small feed of oats or barley with chaff.

A lot of people like to vary the horse's diet because they feel he will eat up better if it contains plenty of interest. For this reason, many traditionalists deplore the whole concept of complete feeds. However, I have no evidence to suggest that my horses enjoy their meals any less simply because they are made up of nuts; if your conscience pricks you, you can always add treats like carrots (chopped lengthwise, to avoid choking), apples, treacle, molasses or carefully selected vegetable peelings.

On balance, complete feeds save the working owner considerable time and worry over the course of the year.

Oats

Oats are enjoyed by all horses and are the most readily digestible of all the basic grains, two factors which have made them the traditional feed. In days gone by, a yard would buy whole oats and crush them to aid digestibility as and when required. Nowadays most oats are bought ready crushed or rolled. Once the kernel has been split the grain starts to deteriorate in feed value, and even more so when the bag has been opened to the elements – a consideration for the one-horse owner feeding oats as only part of the concentrate ration. The oat has 'heating' properties and can literally go to the heads of many animals. It should be fed with considerable discretion to horses being lightly worked on weekdays.

Barley

Barley has become increasingly popular in recent years. It has the same feed value as oats without the heating effect and horses seem to love it in the cooked, flaked state in which it is most commonly sold. When boiled it is especially tempting to the sick or fastidious horse. The cooking of whole barley is a non-starter for the working owner as it needs to be simmered for about five hours before the kernel splits to reveal the goodness inside. There is a school of thought that barley should not be fed in such generous quantities as oats because it has a slightly 'poisonous' effect. However, I have been feeding significant amounts to the same animals for many years without problems.

Maize

Maize is also very tempting and, like barley, is more digestible when bought already cooked and flaked. It is very fattening, however, and as it can over-heat the blood it should not form the staple diet of the normal horse. It is best treated as a supplement to the diet, and because of the small quantities in which it needs to be fed, the one-horse owner may not find it cost-effective. In warm weather it is inclined to go off within two or three weeks if not carefully stored in a cool, dry atmosphere.

Sugar-beet

Occasionally there have been promotions aimed at encouraging the feeding of soaked sugar-beet pulp as a major part of the horse's diet. I have reservations about this idea, first because large quantities readily consumed (horses love it!) can distend the stomach, and second because it can have a laxative effect. However, it is undoubtedly of value, not only for its own content but also for providing roughage, succulence, and for dampening down an otherwise dusty ration. About half a scoop of soaked sugar-beet can be added to each hard feed.

The important thing is that it must be *well* soaked before feeding, because otherwise it may swell in the stomach and cause colic (for the uninitiated, sugar-beet absorbs a staggering amount of fluid), and because fed dry it could choke the horse. The shredded pulp variety should be soaked for 12 hours in three times the volume of cold water, while the more compressed pellet or pulp nut version should be soaked for 24 hours in four times the volume of cold water. The problem here is that because fermentation begins once it is wet, only a day's supply of sugar-beet should be made up at a time, which can result in the one-horse owner fiddling about with very small amounts daily. The temptation to make up a bucketful and use it over two or three days should be firmly resisted. The moment the beet starts to smell vaguely alcoholic it should be thrown away. A common short-cut practised by those who have forgotten to soak the beet overnight is to start it off with hot water. In theory this appears to reduce drastically the soaking time. However, it is potentially dangerous as it accelerates fermentation.

The inclusion of sugar-beet means that your deputies cannot fail to give your horse a dampened feed. However, when making up a day's supply of meals, put the sugar-beet at the bottom and do not mix it until it is to be given. Feeds dampened in advance and allowed to stand become less appetising.

Beans

Soya-bean meal is most commonly fed as a 'neat' addition to a traditional concentrate ration, but both soya and locust bean can be found in compound mixes and nuts. They have a very high protein content – 20 per cent – and for this reason are not normally needed by anything other than top-level performance horses, or brood mares in the last few months before foaling.

Because soya meal, especially, is very dense it should be carefully weighed so that it is not over-fed. Again, beans go off very quickly if left unused so are not suitable for the one-horse owner.

Linseed

Linseed was very popular in the old days and is still so in competition and particularly showing yards as it is fattening and adds gloss to the coat. The problem is that to show any real benefit it has to be fed for at least ten days and as it has to be cooked this may not be feasible for the working owner.

Unboiled linseed can have a poisonous effect. For those with the time, soak a handful of linseed overnight in a saucepan (which should be reserved for this purpose) and next day bring to the boil. Allow to cool, when it should set and then be fed as a jelly mixed with the hard feed.

Bran

Bran has been traditionally fed with the concentrate ration, first to encourage mastication and prevent the ration being bolted down, and second as a tempting 'mash' with a laxative effect – thought to be ideal for a tired horse at the of a long day's hunting or competing in the prevention of colic. Unfortunately, today's milling processes are so efficient that the food value of bran is very low and the lack of wheat flour can turn many peoples' attempts at mash-making into an unappetising-looking, leafy gruel. For this reason it is a hideously expensive way of adding bulk to a concentrate ration.

Bran also has a mineral imbalance; if fed to youngstock it should be countered with a supplement containing calcium.

Chaff

In view of the above remarks about bran, chaff (chopped hay) is a more economical bulk addition to hard feed. Some yards make their own using a chaff-chutter but this is unlikely to be a viable proposition for the working one-horse owner. It can be bought ready cut from feed merchants, usually with molasses added, which makes it more palatable and helps to reduce the dust. You should be aware when purchasing molassed chaff of obscure origins that the molasses may be used to disguise a poor-quality hay content. Watch out, too, for large globules of molasses and mix the whole ration well to avoid choking.

Some new types of chaff have come on the market in the form of herbal mixes, which also fall under the category of supplements. Friends who have used them say that their horses relish the taste and that they kill two birds with one stone. Unfortunately they are expensive and may not be cost-effective if fed with an already vitamin-enriched complete feed.

Supplements

There is an unending and confusing range of supplements on the market, many of which are very expensive. If you are stuck with poor-quality grazing and inferior hay you may be wise to resort to a general mineral supplement to ensure that all your horse's dietary needs are being met. But a great many supplements are aimed at enhancing the condition of the performance horse and their effects may be lost on the ordinary riding animal; if you are already feeding a significant ration of compounded nuts or pre-mixed feed the extra expense of supplements is not justified. One should always follow the manufacturer's instructions to the letter and check to see whether the supplement is a general one or a specialist formula to rectify a particular deficiency – which your horse may not even have. Consult your vet if necessary, and never mix two supplements – they could either react adversely or even cancel each other out. Don't kid yourself that you can economise by feeding less than the

59

prescribed amount; some supplements (such as biotin, now widely available to promote the growth of healthy horn in the hoof) do not work at all unless fed at the minimum ratios specified.

There is so much activity in the horse-feed market that you will often find your local feed merchant has a sales drive on new brands of feed and additives. Don't let yourself be pressurised into trying something new without a free sample. Horses can be surprisingly fussy about changing to a different type of mix, even from the same mill, and over the years I must have thrown away half a dozen sacks of new-style feeds that my horses did not want.

Making up feeds

Most working owners prepare the day's feeds in the morning and leave them for others to feed in their absence. Time can be saved by doing this the night before but water or other dampeners should not be added until it is time to feed. To save others trouble, working owners often leave, say, the horse's tea ready in the manger for when he comes in. This is not such a good idea; first, during the day birds (or, if on the ground, rats) can get in and pick at it; and second, the horse that always expects to find food waiting in his box becomes bad mannered and learns to rush through the door – potentially hazardous for any unsuspecting person bringing the horse in for you. It is best to leave the relevant feed handy near your stable with a lid or upturned bucket on top.

In good yards feed bowls are washed out every day. On hygiene grounds this is a must if they are swopped around between animals. I have never experienced any harm from leaving the individual animal's bowls or manger unrinsed during the week, especially if the horse licks them out well so that stale dregs do not build up in the corners, but they should be properly swilled out with hot water every weekend. Further advice on feeding horses in the field is given elsewhere. Don't forget that buckets, bins or semi-permanent mangers in the field need regular cleaning too; how do you know that your horse hasn't inadvertently splashed urine into them while you were away?

Chapter 5

Mucking out

Mucking out is undeniably the DIY horse-owners' most hated chore. On mornings when you are watching the clock it can seem to take up more time than anything else. Unfortunately, it cannot be skimped without compromising your horse's health and your own costs.

Many people with limited time will, rightly, devote their precious minutes to seeing to their horse's basic requirements of food, water, exercise and warmth and will put mucking out at the bottom of their list of priorities, getting away with a quick skip out during the week, and then having a 'blitz' on the bedding at weekends. This is not really satisfactory. However good the drainage in your stable, and although one can buy specially formulated stable deodorising fluids to spread over the bare floor, neglect of the bedding can still foster ammonia and the spores that cause coughs or other respiratory problems. Additionally, urine-soaked patches not removed daily will spread across the floor – a hideous waste, especially if you use expensive shavings, and it also means that there is more than seven days' worth of soiled under-bedding to remove at the end of the week. It can take the best part of a morning to reinstate a box managed – or mismanaged – this way, and having to make four or five trips to the muck-heap first thing on Saturday morning is hardly the way to put yourself in a good mood for the rest of the weekend. For this reason, although 'deep-litter' bedding (in which soiled bedding only is removed and fresh put on top) is commonly practised by working owners, on grounds of saving time it is not really ideal. It all has to be dug out in the end.

It may sound odd, but it is worth asking the yard manager or an efficient friend for a mucking-out lesson. It is definitely a precise skill that needs to be learned. I have known some people whip through a box in ten minutes and do a more thorough job than others who pick through the bedding for an hour.

Types of bedding

Straw

The traditional and cheapest type of bedding is straw. As with hay, livery owners can often buy it direct from the proprietor, which saves storage and transport costs, but also, like hay, the quality can be difficult to control. The stalks should be a pleasant yellow colour and should not have been unduly flattened in the harvesting process. If straw sticks together in damp slabs it should be rejected. First, this is because it is probably mouldy and will contain the fungal spores that trigger off respiratory disorders; second, because it will take you considerable time to separate the fibres to get an even spread of bedding over the box floor, and even then the squashed, limp stalks will drain ineffectively, adding unnecessary time to your mucking out.

Because straw is so cheap it is favoured by most DIY owners although it has the disadvantage of being more clumsy to handle and transport away from the box than other bedding materials. You need to have a large barrow at your disposal as it is virtually impossible to dump any quantity in skips or plastic sacks. Straw bedding can also make money for the horse-owner, especially in suburban areas where there will be a ready supply of gardeners who want your manure. In livery yards, however, it is not usually the practice to split the proceeds amongst the clients whose horses have contributed to the muck-heap!

Shavings

At up to six times the price of straw per bale, shavings tend to be avoided by those on a budget unless the horse has a wind problem. Shavings only provide a desirable dust-free bedding if they really are *shavings* that have been prepared commercially for horses, albeit at a premium. Local wood mills may sell off their trimmings, full of a mix of sawdust, shavings and offcuts, but this is only suitable if you can spare the time to pick through each load and remove harmful foreign bodies. I once found a 6 inch (15 cm) nail in one load! Some yards will get a large container-load delivered, saving money because the shavings do not have to be baled by the supplier. This saving may be passed on to the client, but on the minus side the collection of loose shavings involves an inordinate amount of work on weekdays; about three barrow loads are equivalent to one compressed bale. If you have to use loose shavings, the most efficient method is to stock up sackfuls by joining forces with a fellow livery client at weekends and take turns to hold open plastic sacks while the other bales shavings into it with a large shallow feed bowl – more efficient per effort than using a shovel.

A shavings bed is by far the quickest to manage on busy weekdays but as the manure from it is not liked by gardeners, owner-grooms may have to find time at weekends to cart it away periodically if there is nowhere suitable to burn it.

Paper bedding

Shredded paper is preferred to shavings by some veterinary surgeons for horses with respiratory disorders, although from the point of view of labour it is slightly more time-consuming to handle and I have found that there is always proportionately more to throw away. Some yards buy a paper shredder and make their own out of old newsprint which can prove highly economical, but again this is an extra chore the working owner can do without. As a rule most livery yards will not keep it in stock for clients.

Peat

Peat is another alternative for horses with wind problems. It is not widely used these days on grounds of expense although it is as easy to manage as shavings. Unfortunately, because it has a deodorising property it can be very tempting for the owner-groom to skimp on the mucking out and he could end up with large patches of wet matter which could set off foot problems like thrush.

Equipment

The right tools make the job of mucking out a lot easier. You should try to use a proper, lightweight stable fork, a big shovel and sturdy, wide yard broom (which obviously sweeps away more waste for your effort than its inadequate domestic equivalent). A pair of stout rubber or other gardening gloves (not washing-up gloves – they tear too easily) are useful. Plastic laundry baskets are popular alternatives to the skip on grounds of cost but they do tend to split after about three months if overloaded and thrown about.

Availability of wheelbarrows is often a thorn in the side for the DIY owner based in a yard with other owner-grooms. Livery yards invariably provide some for clients' use but working owners will inevitably want to use them at the same time. You may consider buying your own but choose carefully – ordinary, garden wheelbarrows are cheap compared with stable or farm barrows (unless you are lucky enough to pick up one at a farm sale), but they are rarely man enough for the job. The capacity is usually too small to cope with the amount of manure and dirty bedding to be removed daily from a single box, usually obliging the user to make two or even three trips to the muck-heap when he should really only make time for one. If you do buy an expensive stable barrow, make sure it has two front wheels which makes it better balanced and easier to handle when fully loaded, rather than simply a large version of the garden, one-wheeled variety.

A compromise, much recommended by a colleague, is a 'ball-barrow', a dustbin-like plastic container which sits on a sturdy football-sized rubber ball. Apart from being roomy enough to accommodate a good box-load of muck, the ball mechanism apparently copes better over rough ground (and generally all types of going except deep snow) than the traditional, narrow wheel. It is ideal for those who have a long trip to the muck-heap – in my friend's case, about 100 yards (metres) from the stables at the front of her house to the other end of her back lawn.

If you are based in a livery yard and decide to buy your own stable equipment and barrows, you must be prepared for others to use or maybe break them while your back is turned, unless you do not mind appearing anti-social by locking them away.

The art of mucking out

When mucking out straw or shavings, first remove obvious piles of dung. Then using a stable fork for straw or, if easier, a shovel for shavings, deftly pick or scrape away the clean bedding to the sides of the box to reveal the soiled matter underneath. This will normally be in the middle, draining towards the slope of the box floor. In makeshift, badly designed boxes (often the lot of the livery owner) be aware of depressions in the floor where liquid can gather and also look to the base of the walls, where urine can accumulate over a period of time and turn the rarely examined bedding into a reeking, solid black mass. Shovel this away into the waiting skip or barrow, and sweep up the remnants so that there is no urine-soaked matter to taint the next bed. The clean bedding is then forked, raked or shovelled back to the middle and further bedding taken in from the sides.

It is a hazard for the horse and also false economy to keep a thin bed. If he kicks the bedding away during the night he could scrape his legs and even end up with capped hocks or elbows. A thicker, more comfortable bed is not only safer but stays cleaner as compacted straw and/or shavings tend to 'hold' urine in smaller patches and reduce the area soiled. A good way to test the depth of the bed is to drive the fork in with some force; if you hear it clink against the concrete or stable floor, the bed is not deep enough.

A lot of people don't bother banking up the sides of the boxes. But banks help to prevent the horse getting 'cast' – jammed on his back or side against a wall – when he lays down or rolls. Horses belonging to working owners and not under twenty-four-hour supervision, because they are kept on premises away from the owner's residence, most definitely need the safeguard of generous banks, which if possible should take up about the same space as a line of straw bales round the base of the walls. If there is not enough bedding left for the banks, then this is where the new straw or shavings should be distributed.

Some yards still follow the old practice of taking all the bedding to the walls to expose the floor during the day and therefore give the box a good 'airing' (this also saves on bedding because the horses droppings obviously do not soil it). I cannot think it is any pleasure for the horse to stand on a bare floor; it either discourages him from taking a rest, or puts him at risk to capped hocks or other leg injuries when he tries to lay down and slips on the bare concrete. Obviously, airing the floor is a good idea if the horse is out during the day, but it does involve a degree of extra work which the working owner may not be able to accommodate.

One of the most time-consuming aspects of mucking out is the picking up of small pieces of droppings that have been kicked round the box at night. If you are unlucky enough to own a 'box-walker', whose droppings are completely churned up in the bedding when you arrive in the morning, you have little choice. (You can, by the way, discourage box-walking by dangling a tyre from the middle of the ceiling just below the horse's head level). However, some people seem to get carried away with this particular chore; many is the time I have witnessed the bizarre sight of owners solemnly picking out walnut-sized scraps of manure with a vast stable shovel when the use of hands protected by rubber gloves would have hastened the task.

If you are a working owner pushed for time it is far more important to make sure that the really soiled, smelly, wet stuff has been taken away, and leave the few odd scraps of semi-dried droppings in the box for a less busy time, however much it offends your sensibilities.

In properly run yards where the horses have all-day attention, droppings are removed almost every hour or so, which conserves the bedding. Obviously the working owner cannot do this. But even when my horse has been 'put away' for me at night I have always found it worth making an effort to visit the yard for a skip out after work. It saves double the amount of time in the morning.

Carting the muck away can take up an inordinate amount of time if the yard is badly laid out or amenities are poor. Certainly the best arrangement from the clock-watcher's point of view is where yards bring a tractor-pulled muck trailer into the middle of the yard, enabling owners to muck out into skips and simply pour the contents away on to the pile. The muck is subsequently driven away by a staff member and emptied on to the muck-heap proper. This not only saves the individual trips to the muck-heap but also absolves him of responsibility for tidiness of the heap on busy weekdays, even if he makes up for it at weekends.

An alternative is the mucking-out sheet – a large, home-made piece of sacking or heavy-duty plastic with a rope drawstring edge, which is laid outside the box. All the rubbish is shovelled on to it and the whole sheet is then drawn up into a bundle which can be slung over the back by the energetic and carried up to the muck-heap (which saves a lot of the secondary shovelling needed when emptying a barrow), or left neatly outside the box for someone to collect later, as can a redundant shavings bag. Those hoping to sell straw-based manure therefore have the packages ready.

My own stables are some distance from both the main yard and the muck-heap. I muck out into plastic bags and if they are not collected for me I will occasionally resort to transporting them in my hatchback. If you try to do this, make sure the bags do not get caught on the catch or other projections; you would be amazed how much can leak out of the tiniest tear.

I have friends who swear that they save much more bedding *pro rata* by using two stables per horse – one a day bed and the other a night bed. This is hardly likely to be a practical proposition for most DIY horse-keepers on grounds of stable rental, but those with spare facilities at home may care to try it.

Very small paddocks, barns or corrals will need mucking out if the animals are not to end up living on a carpet of manure. Unfortunately it should be done every day – which just goes to show that keeping a horse out does not always save time – for if left until the weekend the piles of manure will be kicked around and spread over the area. Quicker than a shovel to pick up a whole pile at a time from an open space with no walls to guide it into place is a gadget that you can easily make, as illustrated. It comprises an L-shaped scoop which you slide under the pile of droppings. You then use a flat piece of wood to push the droppings into it and pop the load into a skip.

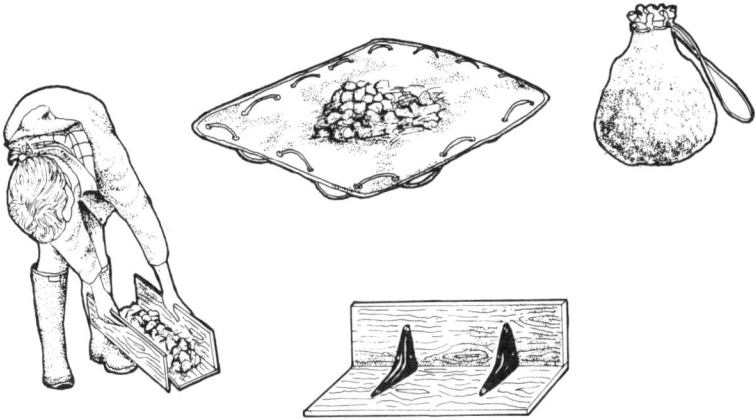

A simple device for scooping up droppings from small paddocks can be made from wood and shelf brackets. TOP: *A mucking-out sheet that can be drawn into a bundle and carried away is a useful alternative to a wheelbarrow.*

Chapter 6
Grooming

Many older manuals on horse-keeping will refer to the necessity of giving a horse a thorough strapping for an hour or more per day – an occupation sometimes more strenuous than the actual riding. Such practices are still advocated by many leading authorities today and certainly there is a strong case in their favour where the fully stabled horse is concerned. But methods of horse-keeping have changed and although many traditional ones are still valid today, the part-time horse-keeper need not feel any shame or inadequacy if he only has time to give his animal a 'lick and a promise' when time is short. In practice, on busy days the working owner can aim to manage with under 10 minutes' brushing per working day, and give the horse two goodish ½-hour sessions at weekends, which ought to keep the stabled animal respectable enough to do you proud in public, clean enough to look okay at performance-type disciplines, though obviously nothing like spotless enough for the hunter show ring.

Why do we groom horses? The most obvious reason is to keep the animal clean – being seen with a scruffy, muddy creature takes a lot of the pleasure and pride out of riding a horse. But more importantly it is to enhance the stabled horse's health by removing the dried sweat and other waste matter from the coat, and also to stimulate the small blood vessels just under the skin and tone up the muscles – just like a massage. So is there a quicker way to do this than to grapple with brushes for 30 minutes or more a day?

A horse that is going out in the field for all or part of the day will appear to demand more grooming than the stabled horse in some ways because, even if rugged and booted, he will still pick up mud and dirt on his limbs in all but dry weather. However, when dry such mud can be swiftly brushed away. In other ways the partly-out horse does not need so much strapping or 'massaging' because the ability to exercise himself at will, denied to the stabled horse, helps to stimulate the circulation and keep the muscle tone right. In these cases attention when grooming in a limited time should be directed to the areas where dirt or dried sweat comes in contact with the tack when the horse is ridden and which could thus rub and foster sores. This would obviously include the head and the saddle and girth area, but don't forget the legs if you boot or bandage your horse. Although not in contact with saddlery, the area between the front legs and beneath the elbows should not be forgotten as, like the human's underarms, it can get sore and nasty if not regularly attended to. The nostrils, eyes and dock should be sponged out daily (using a separate sponge kept specially for the latter). All authoritative textbooks advise washing of the male horse's sheath once a week. I know many people who admit to never doing this mildly embarrassing task, and their horses never seem to suffer ill-effects; certainly some geldings keep naturally cleaner than others, though it can be quite unedifying to catch a whiff of the foul-smelling matter that has been allowed to accumulate. As a compromise for the busy owner I would suggest washing the sheath once every two or three weeks, as it can be quite a task (you often have to wait and catch the horse by surprise when he stales), and you can guarantee non-cooperation if you use cold water as opposed to warm. You should never, ever attempt to wrest the organ from the sheath of a reluctant animal. If you have difficulties, consult your veterinary surgeon, who may offer a mild sedative to relax the animal and enable you to complete the task without fuss.

Traditional strapping involves body-brushing the horse, wisping and going over the whole with a stable rubber to bring up a gloss – almost like polishing a prized piece of furniture, for half an hour or more per day.

The working owner can probably dispense with the wisping and thorough body-brushing as his horse is likely to be turned out during the day and has less need a massage. But the fully stabled horse certainly needs at least 15 minutes' body-brushing on weekdays. You can literally halve the grooming time by forgetting the traditional method of using one brush at a time and cleaning it every few strokes on a metal curry comb held in the other hand. Instead, use a body brush in each hand alternately, brushing in broad strokes in the direction of hair growth (rather like doing the 'crawl' when swimming). The brushes can then be wiped across a metal curry comb strapped to your thigh.

69

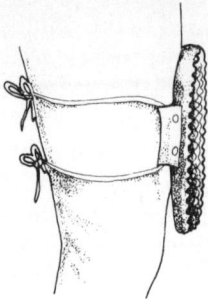

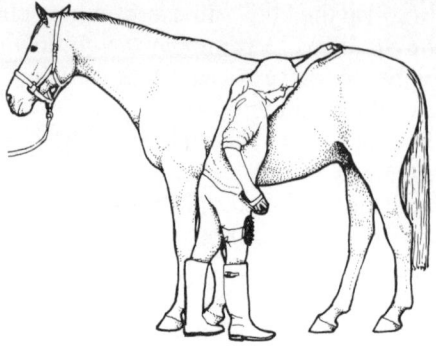

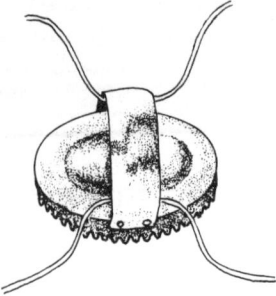

Use of a curry comb strapped to the user's leg; this frees both hands for body brushing and saves grooming time.

A metal curry comb, as commonly sold in Britain, should never be used directly on the horse's coat, although the blunt-edged, oval, metal variety available in Europe is ideal for removing an accumulation of dirt from the horse's trunk area if he has been neglected during the week. The nearest, though less efficient, equivalent in Britain is the plastic or rubber curry comb.

The stable rubber is a much neglected item of considerable use. It is quicker than brushing to remove surface grease and dirt from the head and lower legs. An alternative is a fleecy glove that really picks up the waste matter, although you must then allow time for regular washing of these items. When going to evening jumping shows after work I have found that by removing obvious dirt with a brush and giving the horse a quick rub-over with a fleecy glove I have been able to turn out on a horse that at least looks respectable in the half-light.

Horses' feet must be picked out every day, but unless your horse has particularly dry or weak hooves (in which case veterinary opinion may suggest that there is a deficiency better solved through the feed bowl), there is no need to spend time oiling them on weekdays. The solid type of hoof oil now available is less messy to apply and does not get all over your hands just as you are about to leave for the office. If you apply Cornucrescine, a preparation claimed to promote the growth of horn, the quickest way to wipe it off your fingers is to use a handful of hay; if you try to wash it off you will get in even more of a mess.

Some big yards have electrically operated grooming machines which are doubly labour-saving. They are quick to use and also require less effort to get a good result – the working owner is rarely as fit as the full-time groom. One can also buy brushes and other grooming heads that can be attached to a domestic vacuum cleaner. There are two basic types – a vacuum brush or curry comb that sucks waste matter, loosened by conventional grooming, away from the coat, and the rotary brush. A lot of horses enjoy the bracing massage effect of the latter and it also prepares them for the experience of being clipped, but it can be so efficient that it removes all the protective grease from the coat, for which reason it may not need to be used more than once or twice a week. Take care not to get the rotary brush tangled up with the horse's mane, tail or headcollar rope – some of the older versions do not have an automatic cut-out mechanism in case of jamming. Remember to reverse the direction in which the cylindrical brush-type rotates when you move to the other side of the horse so that you are not brushing against the direction of the coat. The latter can throw out an incredible amount of dust and the user should wear goggles and a mask to protect eyes and lungs. Legislation covering health and safety at work obliges yards to provide these items for staff but they are under no such obligation to supply them to livery clients, who are not employees and are using this equipment by choice. If necessary, you can buy your own mask from a chemist.

Washing horses used to be considered bad practice because it removed too much grease and natural oil from the horse's coat and exposed him to the risk of chills if not properly dried off. Today, washing horses is very much in vogue and I know some competition yards where it has taken over from grooming as the principal means of keeping clean. Except in the emergency circumstances detailed elsewhere, I cannot recommend it to the working owner unless he has a reliable assistant or except in very warm weather. This is because although washing is much quicker than grooming, it takes time to dry the horse off properly. Whereas the full-time horse-keeper can get on with another chore and keep an eye on the drying-off horse – changing sweat sheets half an hour or so later as appropriate – as a rule the working owner will be wanting to get away from the yard. There is therefore the risk that the horse will be turned out or rugged up for the stable while still cold and damp.

Management of the horse's lower legs in the wet winter months is a real problem for working owners. Full-time owners find it difficult enough to keep the legs clean and dry in order to ward off such skin malaises as mud fever and cracked heels. Especially if the horse lives out all year round, the working owner is often tempted to submit to the fight and will often go for days on end without paying any attention to the pastern area, only discovering the sore, broken skin the hard way when his horse lashes out after being unsympathetically brushed at the weekend. These skin disorders come about in the winter because persistent moisture and dampness on the legs softens the skin and separates the upper skin layers, allowing bacteria to penetrate the cells and set up infection. The answer is to dry the legs thoroughly every time the horse comes in – but this can take half an hour or more, which the working owner can rarely spare in the mornings.

If the horse is stabled full-time the best way is to keep the moisture out by applying a barrier cream like Vaseline to the heels and pastern before exercise. The important thing is to make sure that the leg is dry and absolutely clean beforehand, otherwise you are only creating more trouble by trapping beneath it the dampness and any bacteria that may be present. The most effective way to clean and dry the legs, ironically, is to hose the mud from the leg with a jet of water, and then rub dry with towels (you may need several). If, like me, you have limited facilities and no hose, the only safe alternative is to swill lots of *clean* water down the legs and sponge gently; do not on any account try to semi-brush or sponge still wet, muddy legs or re-use dirty water as you can inadvertently rub it into the softened skin and cause even more problems. If power points are available you can dry the legs with a domestic hair-drier – but make sure it is properly wired and safe. Otherwise you will have to towel-dry the legs, and again the towels will need to be clean if you are not to rub dirt back into the skin.

The removal of semi-dried mud is the problem most frequently encountered by working owners whose horses go out during the day and are brought in from the field by assistants before they get home from work. You can ask them to jet-wash and dry the legs for you, but if this is only to be done half-heartedly it may be preferable, from the horse's point of view, to leave the mud on the legs and then tackle the whole procedure from scratch when you arrive at the yard. You can then apply barrier cream to the dried leg before the horse goes out in the morning.

Where does this leave the owner of the horse who lives out

72

all the time in the mud? In my experience the lesser of the evils is to jet-wash out the pasterns and heels daily, rub with a towel to remove excess moisture and then apply a mild, antibiotic non-barrier cream to nip any infection in the bud.

Even these bare minimum treatments will add fifteen minutes to your weekday horse-chore time. If the horse does not seem susceptible to skin disorders you are fortunate, but it is still worth finding the time to take precautions – even if it means riding out on a horse with a dirty neck and tail – as cracked heels and mud fever take a lot of curing, and once a horse has had them they tend to recur. Horses with white legs are more naturally disposed to skin infections and merit special attention.

Chapter 7

Horse clothing and tack

Clothing is necessary for any horse being worked on a regular basis; even the hardy cob-type living out all year round will require a New Zealand rug if only to keep him manageably clean, let alone for the more crucial business of keeping him warm and dry.

Research and innovation in the textile industry has led to horse rugs with thermal, reflective, semi-permeable and numerous other advantageous properties making a big impact on horse clothing. They provide the new horse-keeper with a huge and confusing choice.

When building up a horse's wardrobe from scratch, purchase of a quick-to-fit super luxury rug can save the owner a lot of 'dressing' time and may also be more economical *pro rata* than several cheaper, less efficient stable rugs; some manufacturers claim that their 'high-tech' fabrics will keep the horse every bit as warm as a traditional assortment of jute or quilted rug and under-blankets which seem to take an age to fit when you are watching the clock. However, a lot of these 'new' rugs can be very expensive – around the £100 mark. Bear in mind the necessity for back-up clothing – sometimes rugs will get ripped beyond repair, or so wet that they simply have to be taken off and dried elsewhere. The owner with little time to spare for needle and thread may conclude that it is better to have a larger selection of cheaper rugs and blankets always available.

The bare minimum of clothing required by the fully stabled or part-stabled horse that is to be clipped in the winter, is a New Zealand rug (preferably backed up by a spare), a stable rug, two under-blankets (unwanted bed blankets, duvet seconds and army surplus are a cheap alternatives to purpose-made ones), two cotton sheets (to be worn in the summer and winter next to the skin, to save frequent washing of heavier woollen blankets), and an anti-sweat sheet. The latter is available in two basic types – the traditional 'string-vest' mesh design, which correctly should be used in conjunction with a sheet so that small pockets of air are trapped next to the skin to prevent the horse getting a chill, and the newer type made out of 'high-tech' fabrics that, used on their own, let the moisture out but keep the heat in.

You may get by with just one set of stable bandages (for use for support when treating leg injuries, extra warmth in very cold weather and to double as travelling bandages). Stable bandages are too heavy and cumbersome for exercise so if you want to protect the horse's legs you will need a lighter, more pliable set. Avoid those that are obviously elasticated – ineptly applied they can pull tight and damage the tendon – and don't use Vetrap directly on the leg. (You may well have seen the three-day event fraternity sporting this colourful stuff but they use it in a different context, namely to secure specially moulded tendon guards and other leg protectors for the cross-country phase.)

These days most bandages have Velcro fastenings which are quick and also safer than old-fashioned tapes that you tie yourself. This is because, if incorrectly or hurriedly tied, the knot can sit on the tendon and cause damage if the bandages start to slip or pull taut.

Traditionally, the horse has a separate set of clothing, usually matching, for travelling to shows or hunting, but his ordinary stable wear can suffice as long as you have a change of clothing available in the event of his sweating on the journey. If you are working to a very tight budget you are better to spend your money on the best protection you can afford for his legs and head when travelling rather than splashing out on a smart, monogrammed 'Sunday-best' rug.

New Zealand rugs

So-called because of the country of origin, the New Zealand rug is probably the one garment where one must stress quality rather than economy. Unfortunately the very best rugs can cost two or three times as much as the budget variety, which to the newcomer may not appear particularly inferior. I would recommend buying the very best you can afford, even if it means taking out a small bank loan. The superior makes not only offer the horse better protection from the elements – an important consideration if you can't always get to your horse to bring him in when weather turns bad during your working hours – but outlast the cheaper varieties by several years. If well maintained, the better makes also retain a reasonable secondhand value.

Special features to look for are depth – you should not be able to see the horse's tummy when the rug is in place – and the superior, fitted cut and surcingle-free means of securing, usually via two leg-straps that cross-over between the hindlegs. An alternative is the American cross-surcingle that fits loosely under the girth at a clever angle. These two types of fittings help to avoid potentially harmful, constant pressure on the horse's spine and enable the rug to right itself when the horse rolls. (Rugs secured by surcingles often end up dragged half way round the horse's body, exposing half of it to the elements, as too-tight surcingles 'jam' the rug into the wrong position when the horse rolls.) The best-quality brands use cotton flax for the outer, instead of the cheaper canvas popular on budget rugs. The flax offers superior waterproofing, excellent durability and is less likely to 'snag' or tear against fences or protruding branches.

Alternatively, you can buy New Zealands made from innovative fabrics which are very lightweight, rip-proof, warm and can even be put in the washing machine or tumble-drier, unlike their cumbersome canvas equivalents. My personal experience of this type is limited, though friends who have them enthuse, with perhaps the one reservation that some don't always breathe as efficiently as those made from natural fabrics and that occasionally the horse will sweat up underneath.

A further advantage of the quality New Zealand rug is that it often has accessories – detachable under-blankets and neck covers. These provide extra warmth and are of particular value to the owner who often gets delayed in the office and worries about his horse waiting to come in from the cold. Neck covers made out of the same materials as the rug and lined are especially useful, as *pro rata* you seem to keep in a considerably greater amount of body warmth for the extra amount of the horse's surface area under cover. The disadvantage, however, is if used for more than six hours or so a day neck covers can start to rub and thin out the mane. Neck covers incorporating hoods or covers that go partly over the head and are made out of nylon should be avoided for day-long, unsupervised use; they are aimed at keeping the horse clean rather than warm and, however well fitted and cut, there is always the danger that they will twist round and cover the horse's eyes while you are away.

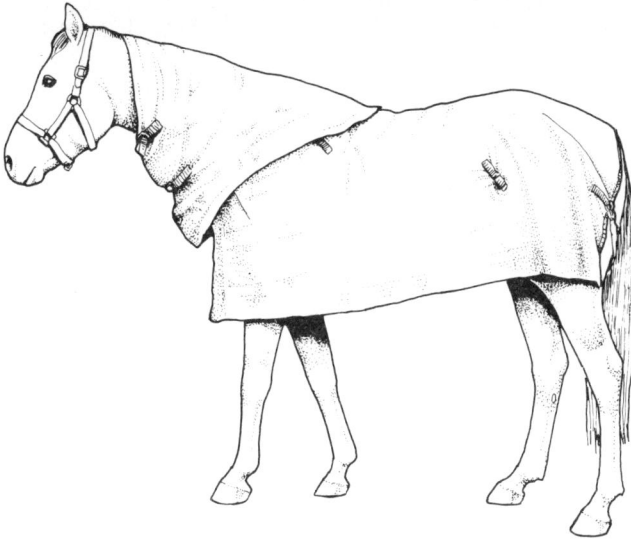

A New Zealand rug with neck cover, which provides significant extra warmth and protection from the weather.

A clipped horse that has to stay out from dawn till dusk because of his owner's working hours will often get cold in the field, even if wearing a rug. Most owners get round the problem by putting extra rugs or string-vest-type sweatsheets underneath the New Zealand, but care should be taken with choice and fitting. Firstly, you cancel out the benefit of a surcingle-free New Zealand if you end up using one to keep the under-rug in place. Secondly, under-rugs not secured to the outer New Zealand can slip back or round during the day, so the poor horse is throttled at the front while the rear of the under-rug protrudes and is exposed to the rain; the wet then creeps up under the New Zealand and you end up with a horse with a wet back. Thirdly, as soon as you add extra rugs you are changing the shape of the horse and the New Zealand leg-straps or other fitting mechanisms need adjusting to restore the supplier's recommended amount of slack; if the leg-straps are too tight they will rub the horse and may break or pull the fittings off the fabric when under pressure (i.e. when the horse rolls).

Over the years I have tried various means of securing non-purpose-made under-rugs to surcingle-free New Zealands, which have included cutting suitable holes through which the leg-straps are threaded, or sewing strong metal rings on the under-rug at

77

appropriate points so that the New Zealand leg-straps clip on these as well as their own ring. Neither of these has proved ideal because, of course, no two manufacturers' rugs are cut the same. During the day they can work themselves into different positions, pull against each other and snag or tear. The most satisfactory make-shift solution (though not cheap and initially time-consuming to set up) is to sew a wide strip of Velcro along the spine of each rug from the wither to the loins. As there is a variable as opposed to fixed point of attachment this allows flexibility when securing one rug to another. Each rug is put on the horse at a 'natural' resting place dictated by its cut and then secured to the one below by the Velcro along the central back seam.

This system can, of course, also be used to save a little time by securing cotton sheets or other under-rugs in the stable. The whole lot can be thrown on to the horse as one unit, although you will still have the front straps to do up. The Velcro system makes the rugs interchangeable, but I would beware of having a spare strip of Velcro next to the horse's coat in case of rubbing.

The drying of flax and canvas New Zealands is difficult for those with limited facilities and shows why it is useful to have a spare. Loading a saturated rug into the back of the car and then trying to hang it up in your kitchen to dry overnight – a common chore for DIY livery owners – without making a mess is not a lot of fun. Common practice is to spread the rug, blanket side down, out over a hay or straw sack, but the outside can still be wet in the morning and unpleasant to put on.

Unless you have an inferior quality rug or one that is so old that it leaks, a rug that is really wet on the outside can safely be left on a horse that is at grass full-time for he will form a layer of warm air between his coat and the rug which, unless disturbed, fulfils the dual function of keeping him warm and the lining dry.

However, some owners short of time have been known to leave a drenched rug on a stabled horse overnight. This may be logical but it is not desirable. It will certainly dry on the animal overnight but, unlike the horse at grass, the stabled animal cannot move round to keep warm and with just a single, clammy rug on, his body temperature may drop, with too much of the heat he produces going to 'air' the rug rather than keep him warm.

The smallest amount of heat will help to dry a rug overnight. Obviously, like any other fabric it should not be hung next to an electric fire. However, I managed to pick up cheaply a small, low wattage free-standing radiator. I suspend wet rugs over it in the garage at home and they are always bone dry in the morning.

New Zealand rugs tend to be thought of as winter wear and are usually stored away in the summer. This is, of course, the time to get any rips patched and the whole rug re-proofed where appropriate. Do not wait until the winter when your local rug repairer – usually contactable through the saddlery shop – has a long waiting list of people who, like you, have left it until the last minute. It is often forgotten that New Zealands can be needed during the English summer. Judicious use can make all the difference when you are trying to run a thin-skinned animal of Thoroughbred type off grass. Even if the weather is relatively mild, Thoroughbreds can get cold, tucked up and miserable in persistent rain, which affects

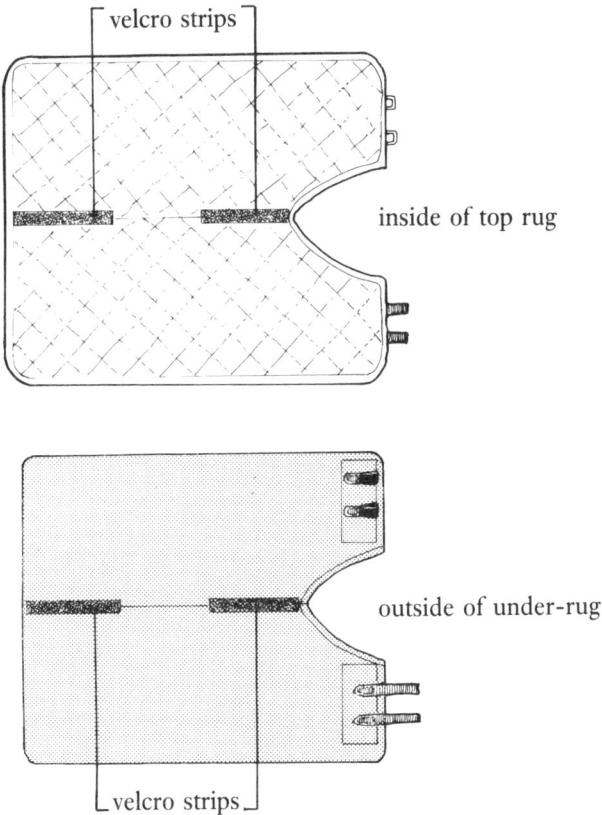

velcro strips

inside of top rug

outside of under-rug

velcro strips

To save time when rugging up and to help stop under-rugs slipping, items of horse clothing can be secured together by stitching wide strips of Velcro along corresponding back seams.

their general well-being. Mine is always happier if he wears his New Zealand at night in wet summer weather. One has to observe a degree of common sense and keep an eye on weather forecasts in case of a heatwave. Generally speaking, if the daytime temperature has been around the 50°–60°F (10°–16°C) mark, the rug goes on at night.

Another advantage of rugging the grass-kept horse in summer is that you can afford to clean him by washing rather than strapping to save time, as the use of the rug means it is less essential to allow grease to build up in the coat to act as protection from the weather.

Stable rugs

There is an immense variety of stable rugs on the market, the choice of which is up to the individual. For the working owner a main consideration is going to be the fitting. Like the New Zealand, you want rugs that do not slip round in the long days and nights when the horse goes without attention. You will also be looking for fittings that are quick to do up – fiddling with three or four front buckles with numb fingers in very cold weather can seem to take forever when you are in a hurry. However, if you go for the quick-fitting plastic-slot variety make sure that replacements can be readily obtained in case of breakages – some horses love to chew them. Some under-rugs are sold without front fastenings, instead being sewn up in front and put over the horse's head. You can compromise with the above in the worst of the winter when several rugs are used to keep the horse warm. Attach them together using the Velcro methods explained above and keep the buckles done up; you can then save considerable time by putting the whole thing over the horse's head as one unit. The points to bear in mind are that you should not go about it like a bull in a china shop – head-shy horses may hate the idea and should be introduced to it gradually. Also, there is a knack to it and even when you think you've cracked it, take a moment to check that the sheets are lying in place and are not crumpled or pulling the coat against the direction of natural growth.

You can save grooming time by regular washing of undersheets or other rugs which lie next to the horse. They pick up a surprising amount of dirt and grease that is otherwise rubbed back into the coat. Some 'high-tech' rugs have thermal properties that stimulate the tiny blood vessels under the skin and actually encourage the transference of waste matter from the coat into the fabric. These rugs need washing once a week if their 'grooming' function is to be exploited fully.

Like New Zealands, stable rugs are now secured by a variety of surcingle-free methods, although the roller is still commonplace.

While wanting to avoid undue pressure, one needs a fairly firm fitting to keep the rugs in place if the horse is to be unattended for long periods in your absence. A satisfactory solution is a stretch roller. The actual roller unit itself, with stretched straps either side, can be bought separately and used in conjunction with a girth. The roller can be done up reasonably comfortably when the horse is normally standing still but when, for instance, he lays down or rolls – the times when rugs are likely to be dislodged – it grips and holds them firmly in place. A pad of foam rubber or Fybagee placed under a conventional roller has a similar effect to the stretch roller. However, such use of foam or other pads cancels out the benefit of the roller by filling up the gullet and pressing on the spine. An anti-cast or 'arch' roller is preferred by some for stabled horses left unattended for long periods. As its name implies, the iron loop over the back deters the horse from rolling right over in his box and getting stuck. However, these are expensive gadgets and the cost may not be justified as many horses turned out during the day tend to do their rolling in the field rather than in the stable.

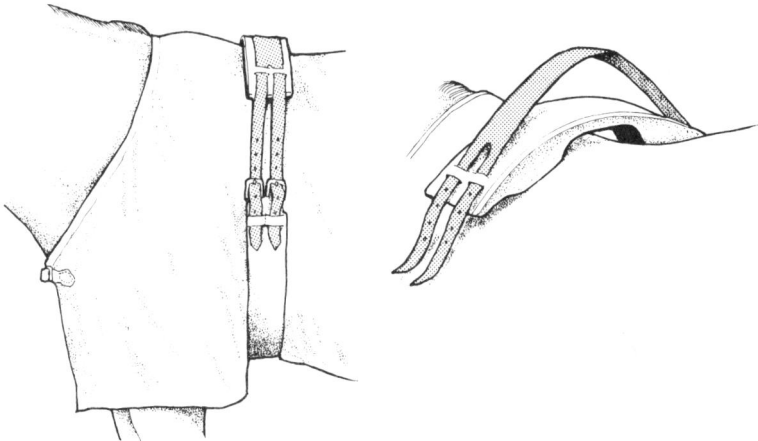

A useful stretch roller attachment: it 'grips' without being tight and helps to keep rugs in place when the horse is unsupervised for long periods.

81

Boots and bandages

Bandages are used on the stabled horse for warmth, which also promotes circulation in the limbs and thus helps to prevent the legs from filling on the horse's return to inactivity from strenuous work.

Apart from fulfilling the warmth factor in bitterly cold weather there is no real place for stable bandages in the working owner's routine. First, ideally the horse will be turned out during the day in your absence and natural exercise will help to keep the legs right. Second, bandages need to be applied skilfully and carefully, not with one eye on the clock. Incorrectly done they can either fall down and get tripped over or, worse still, tighten round the leg and damage the tendons.

For exercising purposes, especially when a horse naturally moves close or when he is doing a lot of gymnastic work which could cause him to strike into himself, boots are preferable when time is short. Boots with Velcro fastenings as opposed to buckles or clips are most popular because they are quick to fit and also because, if broken, the straps can easily be replaced with new Velcro bought off the roll at a haberdashery. Boots are also quicker to wash than bandages, by being dunked in a bucket after use; remember that the insides should always be cleaned as sand and soil can creep up the lining and then get rubbed into the skin, setting up infection or irritation. Boots can also safely be left on a horse in the field during the day although the more solid, plastic or polystyrene moulded type which offer superior shock-absorbing qualities may, on the other hand, rub over a period of time.

Unsupervised horses should not be turned out wearing bandages because of the danger of the bandages slipping or unravelling, damaging the legs or panicking the animal.

One area where I favour bandaging is for travelling. One can buy excellent travelling boots that are easy to fit and protect the leg from top to bottom more effectively than the bandage and Gamgee method. However, when in transit the constant and, for the horse, unpredictable movement of a lorry or trailer exerts incredible stress on the limbs. I therefore would always bandage for *support*, even if using travelling boots on top for extra protection. Assuming that one would normally be travelling a horse at weekends or on a non-working day, the normally busy owner should have time to dress his horse properly for the lorry.

Tack

Although just about everyone now has a webbing girth and headcollar for everyday use, webbing bridles and fabric-covered saddles have been fairly slow to catch on in Britain. For this reason, webbing bridles can often be picked up cheaply in saddlery sales. I use webbing bridles all the time for work, keeping my leather ones for shows. This obviously cuts down tack cleaning and soaping during the week, although one is not completely let off the hook. The bit should always be washed off after use and the straps next to the skin should be wiped to remove any sweat and grime that would otherwise get rubbed back into the horse's cheek and nose next time he is ridden. But at least these two tasks can be done at the same time and with the same cloth. The bridle can be thrown in the washing machine about once a fortnight with other bits of

A webbing/synthetic bridle; it needs little maintenance and saves time on tack cleaning during the week.

horse laundry. When washing any webbing items in a domestic machine it is recommended that you put them in a pillowcase and tie up the top to stop the buckles or other metal attachments causing damage.

Low-maintenance fabric-covered saddles from Australia are beginning to make an impact in the northern hemisphere but they represent a large extra expense on top of a normal leather saddle for 'best'. Use of cotton numnahs and inexpensive fleecy synthetic seat-savers keeps the saddle clean and you can get by with soaping the saddle only at weekends when time is short. But even if the leather looks clean you must observe the discipline of soaping or oiling the leather regularly, not only to preserve your investment but to keep it supple and ward off the dryness that causes splitting or cracking and makes the saddle a dangerous piece of equipment. The weekend is also your chance to inspect stitching of stirrup leathers and girth straps, a crucial safety measure frequently overlooked or put off when time is short.

Chapter 8
Thoughts on fitness

It is much easier to keep a horse fit than to get it fit in the first place. Today, thanks to scientific research and clinical trials, top trainers and competition riders have an advanced knowledge of how to put the edge on their horses' fitness to enable them to perform to their full potential. But, with few exceptions, our proven competition riders still recognise the value of traditional long, 'slow' work in walk and trot – again mimicking nature – to put the foundation on fitness, before they start to top it up with interval training and the like.

This foundation work usually takes place over a six-week period, building up to two hours or so a day. Therefore it can be seen that, unless the working owner has help with weekday exercising, he cannot follow the full-time horse-keeper's practice of giving his horse a long holiday – or to 'let it down' to use the popular term. This is because the daily time commitment involved in bringing a horse in soft condition back to work can be twice that needed merely to maintain the muscle tone and the efficiency of the vital organs that have been carefully and systematically built up.

The working owner who wants to keep his horse competition or hunting fit will almost certainly have to reconcile himself to the fact that he ought to ride his horse three or four times during the week, albeit for short periods of up to an hour, all the year round, give or take a two-week break for your own holiday. This is another major commitment that warrants careful consideration if horse-keeping is being considered for the first time.

Work to get a horse fit for the tasks intended, as opposed to exercise merely to maintain health, has to be regular and cumulative. You cannot make up for leaving the horse idle during the week by going for a couple of three-hour 'burn-ups' on Saturday and Sunday. A problem for the inexperienced rider is that it is in the horse's nature, especially with better-bred, hot-blooded types, to keep going even when he is physically tired. This strong influence of 'mind over matter' can often be experienced on the way home from such excitable outings as a day's hunting. The horse will jig-jog all the way back to his box even though logic suggests that he must be exhausted. Unfortunately this behaviour can mislead the less knowledgeable owner into thinking that his horse is fitter than he really is, and as a result he may be encouraged to overdo it at weekends. Over a period of time, persistent hard work at weekends without maintenance exercise in between will cause undue wear and tear of the muscles, ligaments and vital organs. The result can be lameness and respiratory disorders which cost money to cure. And once a horse has got a 'leg', unsoundnesses do tend to recur, even with thoughtful management. Over-stressing inadequately prepared limbs and organs can shorten the horse's working life.

This does not, of course, mean that you cannot go out for long rides or take your horse to shows at weekends if he has done little apart from idling about the field during the previous five days! The prospect of riding at weekends is of course the main inspiration for many of us to struggle through the mud in the dark, caring for our animals in the long winter months. The half-fit horse can certainly handle a day at a riding club show or a 2-3 hour hack *as long as he is treated with respect.*

Half-day hacks can be safely undertaken *if* you limit your trots and canters to the best going, allow plenty of recovery periods at walk in between, stop for a 15-minute rest at some stage or at least get off and lead him for a short while to relieve his back – and your legs too, if you aren't really fit. Likewise, if you are hacking to a show, allow plenty of time to get there so that you don't have to trot all the way in order to make the first class, and don't ride round the showground unnecessarily or treat your horse as a mobile chair between events. (It should go without saying that this is the best way to conserve the energies of the fit horse too.)

Fitness is a complex subject and it is beyond the scope of this book to explain it in detail. There follows suggestions about the minimum weekday exercising requirements to maintain the conditions of the *already fit* animal, using my experience with my own Thoroughbred and cob as a yardstick.

The Thoroughbred or near Thoroughbred, turned out during the day, needs a minimum of 45 minutes' work on four, or if pushed, three weekdays (usually having Monday off) to maintain the condition that enables him to cope with show jumping, dressage or 2-hour hacks at weekends without unnecessary stress. This work

86

Getting off and leading for 10-15 minutes will preserve the energy of the semi-fit horse on long weekend hacks.

usually comprises about 20 minutes schooling or lungeing followed by a quick hack round the block for a change of scenery and to help him cool down. My rather more stuffy cob, doing the same weekend work, needs a minimum of 1-1¼ hours daily to complete the same weekend tasks. This is partly because nature did not equip him for athletic work quite as well as the Thoroughbred breed, whose better developed blood vessels distribute the oxygen round his body rather more efficiently when in strenuous work. It is also because being rather more laid back and also extremely greedy, the cob, like many other more 'common' horses, is inclined to spend all his time in the field tucking in to the juiciest grass. In contrast, his sprightly Thoroughbred companion wants to play and canter about, thus exercising himself to some degree.

If the already fit Thoroughbred is required to do something more strenuous at weekends – cross-country, hunting in a less fashionable, non-galloping country, or novice level eventing – again my personal experience suggests that the minimum weekday maintenance requirement is increased to 1¼ hours, which would include a good ½ hour in trot and canter in the school, combining training with fitness work, a hack out and a 15-minute cooling-off walk back to the box. I would also try to fit in a 5-minute canter out in the open twice a week – probably on the Tuesday or Wednesday, and the day before the event itself, which would include a strong gallop as a pipe-opener. Again, for the cob the requirement is proportionately longer.

Although some seem to manage it, I cannot see how the horse

owner with a full-time job can get a horse fit and properly trained entirely unaided for competitive disciplines that are both more strenuous and technically demanding than these (intermediate or advanced level eventing and long-distance riding being examples), unless this is to the detriment of their job, the smooth running of their home, and their own health – not to mention that of the horse. The physical demands of these top, tough disciplines involve an incredible amount of work; it has to be sustained over a season and it does not leave the working owner much time to get himself physically fit and mentally adjusted. At this level of competition even top full-time riders, who are in the saddle training for many hours a day, still find they have to undertake extra fitness work of their own – such as jogging, swimming or weight training. They recognise the need to keep hard, sharp, and alert so that they help their horses instead of hindering them. It should be borne in mind that mere participation in and completion of these more demanding disciplines depends on almost scientific study of the finer points of equine fitness over a long period of time, combined with experience which the newcomer cannot hope to grasp straight away.

The fully stabled horse presents rather more of a tie. Irrespective of his weekend activity, he needs at least two hours a day out of his box to compensate for lack of freedom – to maintain health and to keep him entertained. From the point of view of increasing fitness, two consecutive hours' work is probably more effective than an hour before work and an hour after, although the latter may work better with the owner's domestic and business commitments, and also has the benefit of breaking up the stabled horse's relatively dull day.

Ironically, in view of the above observations, a competent rider with even moderate hacking country available can end up getting the stabled horse almost *too* fit. The working owner will have to show particular diligence and ensure that he feeds the horse according to the work required, rather than the other way round – working the horse to use up the excess energy supplied. If necessary the horse should be let down a little, even if you are working towards a competitive goal, because an over-fit, fully stabled horse is susceptible to both physical and mental problems that are difficult for anyone to cope with, let alone the person with a full-time job.

First, the physical problems arise if, say, due to the owner's sickness or a spell of freezing weather, the hard fit horse is suddenly holed up in his box for two or three days. The next time he is ridden he may fall victim to azoturia or 'tying up' – a painful cramp with dramatic symptoms, resulting from renewed stress on muscles that have not been kept in work, as explained elsewhere. The mental problems come because, with fitness, the horse also tends to become more alert and brighter than usual. He is thus much harder to keep entertained, and to keep out of mischief – he may resort to chewing his rugs or developing other vices associated with boredom during his long day in confinement without even human attention. The super-fit horse can also be difficult to feed as he is inclined to go off his bulk intake.

How and where you ride can make as much difference to your horse's fitness as how long and how fast you ride. Undulating country and plenty of hill climbs will improve the efficiency of wind and limbs far quicker than a stroll round flat terrain; a horse made to walk out properly on the bit will muscle up quicker as he has been made to use his back and hindquarters properly, as opposed to the horse who has been allowed to trot on a long rein with his hocks back in the next county. The former comes with riding skill, however, and does not quite fit into the brief of this book. Working on a sand school, rather than on shavings or grass, will also require more effort per stride by the horse – rather like tightening up the tension of the pedals on a human's exercise bike. However, very heavy sand can exert undue stress on joints and ligaments and authoritative advice should be sought before subjecting the half-fit animal to this treatment.

The owner of the fully stabled horse should always be aware of his responsibility towards the fit animal's sanity in his absence; providing a nice big haynet for him to pick at while you are away may not always be enough to overcome boredom during the long hours you are away. Some people provide stable 'toys' for their horses. An inexpensive and frequently relished distraction is a clump of freshly dug turf; after eating the grass some horses have untold hours of simple fun nosing through the sod.

As mentioned elsewhere, one way to maximise the horse's exercise time is to make an arrangement with a like-minded, competent, fellow livery owner and take it in turns to lead each other's horse out on exercise while the non-riding owner stays behind to do both horse's chores. This way each horse gets, say, two hours' exercise a day instead of just one. Advice on riding and leading is given in the chapter on safety.

The horse-walker provides a similar service, but such machines are not a viable proposition for most one-horse owners and are not yet readily seen in ordinary livery yards. Horse-walkers are often described as labour-saving gadgets, but this is a slight misnomer in the context of amateur horse-keeping. Certainly they are labour-saving in professional training or competition yards where exercising horses is a means to an end rather than a joy in itself. For the working owner who keeps his horse for pleasure there is hardly any logic in putting a horse on a walking machine simply to give yourself extra time to fiddle about with the mucking out! For this reason, unless I wanted to top up the horse's fitness in addition to the daily riding I was able to fit in myself, I would not feel tempted to move to a yard simply because it had a horse-walker.

Chapter 9

The daily routine

Planning a weekday timetable is a difficult task for the working owner. Although specimen timetables appear at the back of this book, they represent only a few of the seven or eight different systems I have tried during the twelve years that I have kept horses on other peoples' premises. I am in no doubt that others will have found even more efficient ways of doing things. The only constant factor that we would probably all agree on is that at least three hours each weekday has to be put aside to fulfil one's basic obligations to the part-stabled horse. (On the plus side, two horses take up less time *pro rata*; for instance, it takes the same amount of time to bring in two horses from the field as one, or to empty a barrow containing two lots of evening skippings-out, or to exercise two well-behaved horses together using ride and lead.)

How these three hours are split before and after work will depend on your horse's temperament and metabolism, your working hours and domestic commitments, the availability of turn-out facilities, whether or not it is appropriate to ride morning or evening, and any rules and conditions laid down by the people who own or run the premises you rent. With respect to the last, although few yards will deny access outside certain hours, there may be disquiet if you want to feed at completely different times to the other owners, as this will always upset the other animals.

Another factor which plays a part in deciding on a routine is how good you are at getting up in the morning. Traditionally, staff of professionally run yards rise at dawn, if not earlier, for an early start (no wonder so many horsy jobs involve 'living in'), and many working owners will probably do the same simply to enjoy as long a ride as possible and leave plenty of time to complete stable chores before setting off for the office.

However, unless there are other people and horses to consider, there is no practical necessity to do this in the summer months, nor for those with use of floodlit indoor schools or manèges. Working owners should not feel obliged to get up at 5 a.m. just because it is the 'done thing'. I have several friends who are notoriously bad risers and don't get to their horses until about eight each morning, allowing just half an hour to feed, turn out and organise sundry help for the day before setting off to work. But by the evening these natural night-birds are firing on all cylinders, thoroughly looking forward to spending the evening with their horses when others might want to put their feet up. They can ride without having to watch the clock and claim that mucking out and filling haynets at half past eight at night is the perfect antidote to a stressful day in the office. This may be an unorthodox routine – but it is still a routine and that fulfils one of the golden rules of horse-keeping; not surprisingly their horses flourish on it.

Certainly one can accustom one's body to getting up very early every day, and many of us don't have any choice. But as the double life of the working horse-owner means he has a particularly long day, it cannot be wrong to make it conform where possible with your bio-rhythms. If you persistently force your body to leap into action when it is not ready, you will arrive at the yard at a relatively low ebb, leaving yourself open to greater risk of error because you are not fully alert, and then set off for work feeling fractious even before the day's toil has begun. This is hardly the way to endear you to the person who pays the salary that keeps your horse.

Horses are acutely sensitive to atmosphere and their well-being can be noticeably affected by good or bad 'vibes'. If your horse is going to see you for only a few hours each day, it is surely in the interests of both parties that you are feeling at your best physically and mentally. If that time is in the evening, don't let tradition shame you into thinking it is bad horsemanship.

The best way to organise a timetable is to decide whether you are going to ride morning or evening, work out how to fit everything round it and then stick to this. Some people believe it is better to vary the time of day that you work the horse, to prepare him for the shock to his routine when he goes hunting or to a show (some indoor jumping fixtures, even club shows at local centres, can go on to midnight). My own experience suggests that horses clearly know the difference between 'home' and 'away', and while they adapt, to a point, to unusual hours of eating and standing in the lorry at the latter, at home they work and settle down for the day much better if they know exactly when they are going out or when the next feed is coming.

92

The advantage of riding in the morning before work is, of course, that it starts the day off with a swing and, from a more practical point, a chore crucial to the horse's well-being is out of the way. Horses certainly tend to be in a better frame of mind once they have been out, and an early ride enables feeding patterns to conform to the norm, as the horse does not have to be denied too much bulk during the day because of having to wait for early evening exercise. During the winter the morning is the only time you can hack out in anything approaching daylight hours. If you are based in a commercial yard, generally it will also fit in better with the routine of the people on whose help you may depend for the rest of the day.

The disadvantage of pre-office riding is that if you allow too tight a timetable you end up watching the clock so much that you may have to restrict yourself to the same boring hack round the block, even when daylight hours are on your side. Alternatively, you may find your enjoyment reduced because you put off trying to progress with your horse's flatwork or jumping in case you run into a problem that you cannot find time to work through because you are supposed to be at your desk in 45 minutes. As mentioned before, horses are extraordinarily sensitive to 'vibes' and any rushing or brusqueness on your part, the reason for which your horse cannot possibly understand, can put a slightly nervous type on edge. You have then sown the seed for a 'scene' that could throw out your timetable for the rest of the morning.

Riding in the evening solves many of these problems, but again your regime can be disrupted if you unexpectedly have to work late, or rely on public transport which is cancelled or delayed. If your horse is in a big yard, he may easily be upset at the sight and sound of other horses being given their night-time feeds and hay when he is denied his because you are planning a 6 p.m. hack. Unless you are based in a commercial riding school that has a lot of evening business and whose horses are geared to this, you may also find yourself alone late at night and responsible for shutting up everything before you leave, or, alternatively, being hurried by a tired member of staff who wants to go home rather than wait for you to finish. Obviously, too, much depends on the rider's own temperament and the demands of his work. I enjoy a relaxing hack out in the evening, but if I have had a hard day I know from bitter experience that schooling after work is not a good idea – I rarely have any patience left for my horse.

Using as a model a hypothetical owner who works a regular

8-hour day, taking partial responsibility for his horse kept at premises away from home, we now look at ways in which the basic necessities of horse care can be slotted into two visits a day, firstly for the horse kept under the combined system, and secondly for the horse kept fully at grass.

The combined system (horse stabled at night, turned out during the day)

Morning
On arrival at the yard the horse owner's first task should be to check the horse over for any injuries sustained during the night (or maybe even in the field the day before, but which went unnoticed when he was brought in) and take action accordingly.

Always find time to look for any clues which may suggest ill-health or mismanagement. Scraps of food still in the manger could be last night's supper, unfinished because the horse is feeling off-colour. It could also be this morning's breakfast, unfinished because the person who promised to feed your horse very early forgot to do so and has only just put it in. If the latter is the case the horse must have at least an hour to digest it, which means you may not have time to ride; this is one reason why most DIY owners elect to feed their own horse's breakfast *after* they've ridden, even if it is later than the norm.

For those who feed soaked hay which has to be placed in the stable before leaving for work, it is usually necessary to drain the haynet (left soaking overnight) immediately upon arrival, as it will need at least an hour to drain properly unless you want to mess up your bedding.

It is also usually prudent to pick up the as yet undisturbed piles of droppings at this stage, even if you leave the main mucking out until later, as again inspection can alert you to ill-health. Droppings of the part-stabled, hay and corn-fed horse should be brownish-yellow or brownish-green in colour, depending on access to grass, and formed in fist-sized balls that crumble as they hit the ground. If the consistency is unduly loose or hard it is a sign of possible illness and you should try to determine if anything is wrong before you go rushing off on your ride. Whole pieces of corn – such as oak husks – in the droppings also suggest that something is amiss with the digestion, because as we saw earlier the horse's bowels are very thorough. It is also prudent to pick out the feet at

94

this stage; feeling the temperature of the hooves could alert you to any possible lameness. This quick daily assessment will take only a couple of minutes.

Over the next couple of hours you are going to need a fair bit of equipment from four or five different sources. Time and motion analysts would have a field day in most yards as the amount of time people spend walking between stable, muck-heap, tack room, barn and feed store can be incredible: I once worked out that I wasted up to 15 minutes in every hour doing just this. The obvious but so often overlooked solution is to acquire a small flat-bed trolley, which can often be bought quite cheaply at a farm sale or junk shop (or failing that a clean wheelbarrow that it not used for mucking out). Stack everything you are going to need on to it – your horse's breakfast, change of rugs, grooming kit, tack, your hat and change of boots where required and park it outside your box for easy access.

Some people prefer to get the mucking out done first but I feel it is better to ride, as in a real emergency the mucking out can be skimped or even left if you are delayed on your ride for any reason. The amount of grooming you do will depend on how dirty your horse is and whether you strapped him the night before (further advice given elsewhere), but in any event you should brush the

Equipment stacked on a flat-bed trolley to save time walking back and forth to the tack room and feed shed.

areas that will be in contact with the tack to avoid rubbing and soreness – i.e. the head, saddle area, girth and, if the horse is to wear boots or exercise bandages, the legs. A quick flick-over an already clean horse should take less than 5 minutes, and the tacking up another 5 minutes, so the efficient operator can aim to be on the horse's back within 15-20 minutes of arriving at the yard.

It is not my intention to be a killjoy, but when deciding how or where to ride in the morning the working owner should remember that he does have a responsibility to his employer. You have every right to indulge in risk sports at weekends and in your legitimate free time but on weekday mornings anything unduly reckless that could cause you to be late for work, or maybe have to miss it altogether due to injury, should be avoided. By all means have a jump in the manège – but don't go for an early morning cross-country school. And if you hack out, don't go into a remote part of the countryside on your own; if you have an accident it could be hours before anyone finds you.

Of course, however diligently you plan your pre-work riding, something can go wrong, and advice on how to cope with unexpected problems is given in the next chapter. Nonetheless, you should always allow enough time to bring your horse back to the yard cool, calm and collected, not rushed and in a puffing, sweaty heap, as he will be too stressed and upset to eat his breakfast and is unlikely to be the obliging animal you need if you are always racing against the clock. If you are also going to have to do your own mucking out and turn out, you should aim to finish your riding and have the horse back in the yard a bare minimum of 45 minutes before you have to leave for the office.

Assuming you return to the yard with a calm, dry horse, it should not be necessary to brush him off as, if he is going straight out in the field, he will almost certainly roll and this will remove the itches. He can be untacked, and put straight into his New Zealand rug, when appropriate, which should take less than five minutes. He can then be given his breakfast while you do the mucking out (see Chapter 5). Conveniently, many horses take about 15 minutes to clear up an average breakfast – about the same time as it will take an efficient operator to muck out a box and empty the barrow. You can then turn the horse out, leaving about 15 minutes to complete the remaining essential chores – filling the water buckets, hanging up a haynet prepared the previous evening if the horse is to be brought in for you, and setting up the day's feeds to be given in your absence.

The time the horse comes in at night will be dictated by many factors – the availability of help, the time the owner can get away from work, the weather, and any rules or restrictions laid down by those who are in charge of the yard. Generally speaking, in all but cold, wet weather the horse who expects to come in is generally happy to stay out in the field until dusk. During the summer, therefore, the owner can leave the horse out until after work, but from October to November onwards he should arrange for someone to bring the animal in to a haynet late afternoon, even if they do not change rugs or give a hard feed. More often than not, in the winter months the horse that has been out since 8 or 9 a.m. will be more than ready to come in from about 3 p.m. onwards and will stand in the mud by the gate, cold and shivering. If you cannot arrange this, the horse's outdoor clothing should take into account his getting cold when he stops moving about, especially if he is clipped; as discussed elsewhere, a single New Zealand may not be enough.

In the evening it is always nice for the horse to walk into his box and find a haynet, but for safety reasons, as mentioned elsewhere, I would not leave a hard feed already in the box; this only encourages the horse to rush and if a relative stranger is bringing the horse in he could be caught unawares by a 'barger'. He should be brushed off, his muddy legs attended to where appropriate, and he should be rugged up for the evening, which will take about 15 minutes. If it is dark when the owner arrives I would strongly recommend inspecting the legs for cuts or wounds with a torch or similar direct light source, as the artificial overhead light of most stable lighting has an alarming tendency to 'hide' injuries on non-white legs; twice I have failed to notice quite serious wounds because of this and by the morning infection had had a 12-hour head-start.

Some people recommend giving the hard feed as the owner leaves, so that the horse can eat it in peace. I prefer to feed it earlier, while I do the other chores, so that I can be assured the horse is tucking in and is not feeling off-colour, and so that non-fixed feed bowls – a possible hazard – can be removed from the stable before the owner leaves for the night.

Weekday evening chores will include skipping out the box if the horse has already been got in (up to 5 minutes), preparing tomorrow's haynets (2-10 minutes, depending on whether it is fed 'dry' or has to go into a soaking trough which needs filling), topping up the night's hay supply where appropriate (about 2 minutes) and setting up the next day's feeds and sugar-beet if so desired (about

5 minutes). If the owner's post-work visit is to be the horse's only attention that night he should certainly have two water buckets to last him over the next 12 hours; these should be placed in opposite corners of the box so that if the horse does a dropping or kicks bedding into one of them, he still has a source of palatable water. Optional cleaning of one set of tack need take only 10 minutes, so if there are no problems the owner-groom should be able to get away from the yard within 50 minutes of arrival.

At the weekend

The weekend is, of course, in theory, one's chance to catch up on all the stable tasks neglected during the week, although I would hope that this book shows why it is necessary to carry out certain tasks every day and how to minimise the time needed to complete them properly. However, certain things can reasonably be left till the weekend without disrupting the working owner's entire Saturday. These include a thorough grooming (30 minutes) and tack cleaning (15 minutes), a weekly scrub-out of water buckets and feed bowls (5 minutes), and shaking out of the two or three bales of hay to be used in the next five weekdays to pick out foreign bodies (10-15 minutes).

Many DIY working owners opt for deep-litter bedding, which saves time during the week but often requires an hour or more's extra digging out and multiple barrow emptying at weekends. In Chapter 5 I have discussed the advantages and disadvantages of this system and explained my personal preference for proper daily mucking out, even when time is short. However, for those using either straw or shavings bedding there is a strong case for taking an extra 20 minutes or so on Sunday evenings to put in two additional bales of bedding (much of the excess being taken up by generous banks), which can be absorbed into the bedding during the week as soiled portions are removed. This will save the owner time fetching replacement bedding from the store.

The weekend is also the time to wash horse clothing for those who have limited supplies and who need to put the same rugs back on the horse that night. A summer sheet on a horse that is being brushed off as opposed to strapped will get very grubby and greasy and should be washed once a week, as should a numnah. Beware of overloading a domestic washing machine; if packed too tightly it cannot do its job and the load may not be adequately rinsed, which could prove harmful as some horses have been known to suffer skin allergies when biological powders have been used. The average domestic machine can only cope with one lightweight quilted rug, one numnah and one set of bandages per load.

The horse at grass

A great many people keep their horses entirely at grass, which in the winter saves money and physical labour – but not necessarily a significant amount of time. The working animal that is clipped and New Zealand-rugged will probably need more hard feed than his stabled peer for warmth. Even if he is at grass livery at an establishment where hay is put out in the field as part of the service, the working horse will need hard feeding night and morning – i.e. before and after the office, and this responsibility usually falls to the owner; furthermore, if the horse shares a field then he will either have to be supervised while he eats or be taken out of the field temporarily. Either way this takes up about an extra 40 minutes of the owner's time every day – and this is pretty unproductive, as the owner will have few other essential chores to carry out and will probably end up standing around twiddling his thumbs while the horse cleans up his feed.

A great many horses that winter in either fully or as part of the combined system live out during the summer months, and with *careful* management there is no reason why they cannot be successfully prepared for competition work or similar strenuous activity, even evented up to novice BHS level off grass. Keeping a horse at grass during the summer is certainly a time for the working owner either to enjoy even more riding, with so many daylight hours at his disposal, or to take a pull and use the time saved on stable work to do other things as well. However, although the summer is a time to save money – no hay, less feed, less labour to pay for and maybe saved stable rental too – the owner who wants to keep his horse fit cannot necessarily bank on saving time; his horse will almost certainly still need two visits a day.

Deciding whether or not you can justify just one visit to your grass-kept horse per day depends on the temperament and metabolism of the horse, the availability of extra help to do simple check-overs or straightforward tasks like bringing in and turning out, the work you expect the animal to do and the quality and quantity of the grazing. In some ways it is easier to manage a horse's diet in the winter, for most reasonable livery establishments will put a decent maintenance supply of hay in the grass liveries' field at night and probably morning too, leaving the owner to make

99

up the balance himself with hard feed. But in the summer there may be too much grazing for obesity-prone cob types, obliging the owner to bring the horse in during the day (and thus causing some mucking-out work and the rental of daytime stabling, and thus the necessity for two visits). Alternatively, if the grazing is very poor then the aspirant competition animal again may have to stand in during the day just to be topped up with his own private hay supply. And even if the animal seems to keep his figure, the grass-kept horse that is to be worked strenuously should be brought in and off grass for at least two hours before he is due to be ridden for the sake of his respiration and digestion. When working my lapsed eventer in this way, I usually gave him at least four hours off grass before going for a canter to be on the safe side. Again, the working owner anticipating an after-office ride may have to bring his horse in during his lunch break if he cannot persuade someone else to oblige mid-afternoon.

For those who choose to ride before work in the summer months when the horse on good grazing will be fairly grass-full, the safest thing is to allow yourself at least 2¼ hours when aiming for a 1-hour-plus ride. Having caught him up you can spend around 20 minutes brushing off and tacking up, and then devote at least the first 30 minutes of your ride to walk and perhaps a relatively sedate trot. This gives your horse about an hour to 'deflate' – although this is barely enough if you hope to canter over a sustained period, or to jump. You should also allow at least 25 minutes to untack and hard feed the horse and get him back in the field before leaving for work.

At this time of year it is often preferable to ride in the evenings, obviously because there is less pressure to hurry away and because, if necessary, you may be able to get a 'bloated' horse in from the field on your way home and return later to ride.

The joy of keeping a horse out in the summer is that it matters far less if you visit him at varying times, and your horse's fitness and well-being will not suffer greatly from missing exercise on odd days. However, when you choose not to ride you cannot always afford to award yourself a day off from visiting the animal completely. Even if someone else will take responsibility for seeing that your horse is still on four legs, others will rarely take on the tasks, free of charge, of bringing in the animal when the weather is very hot, or applying copious amounts of repellent lotion when the flies are at their worst.

Getting the horse out of extreme heat and flies in high summer is a particular worry for the working owner, for he can rarely tell first thing in the morning how bad they will be. I work in an air-conditioned office and have often been horrified to emerge into stifling evening heat, wondering what on earth my poor animals have had to put up with during the day. Bringing the horse in before you go to work and turning him out again on your way home is rarely 100 per cent satisfactory, for often the flies do not come out till about noon and can be particularly bad in high summer up till about 9 p.m., neither of which times conveniently correspond to the standard working day. Horses left out all day without adequate shade or shelter can suffer terribly from flies. Apart from the irritation they can inadvertently injure themselves trying to kick them away. Also, persistent stamping on hard ground is bad for the limbs, and I have even known animals to rip off shoes during a frantic gallop round the field trying to get away from the torment. The only solution, though not necessarily the cheapest, is to resign yourself to applying daily one of the long-lasting applications now available, or alternatively to buy one of the permanent fly-repellent tags which can be attached to headcollars. Some friends of mine report good results from tying two or three cattle tags in the mane of horses summering at grass. Fly-repellent lotions need choosing with care; the effects of most of the cheaper brands last only a few hours and they are thus not suitable for horses whose owners cannot get back to reapply them during the day. The products that claim to last several days are the most expensive but their cost can be justified as in my experience they do work for at least one day. Application of such lotions should be done with care and you should allow at least 5 minutes per horse. Aerosol sprays are loathed by most animals; a more efficient and less frightening applicator is the puffer type, commonly sold for gardening use. Lotions of any kind should not be sprayed direct on to the head, but applied carefully with a cloth, and in any case not immediately above the eyes.

If you are riding an 'out' horse in the winter before work you should allow about 20 minutes to get him ready once caught, and another 25 minutes to feed him his breakfast, replace his rugs and get him back out in the field. As detailed elsewhere it is rarely necessary to completely clean a horse for normal hacking, though removal of mud from essential areas like the head, girth, saddle patch (if unrugged) and legs always takes more time than you think. Riding a grass-kept horse after work is virtually a non-starter for those who keep their animals at DIY livery with others. Even if a floodlit manège is available, the normal practice of putting out the evening hay around 4 or 5 o'clock effectively prohibits the owner from riding unless he wants his animal to miss his share of the hay. If your own horse is a shy feeder and vulnerable to bullies, and other owners want to feed in the field before your arrive and you doubt the efficiency of their supervision, it is usually best to leave a token feed comprising a lot of inexpensive bulk feedstuffs to be given your horse. You can then remove him later for his feed proper.

Even if your horse is such a good doer that he survives on hay and is not being ridden, he should still be caught up once if not twice daily for an overall check and, where appropriate, to have his rugs straightened. I, like many others in a rush, often do just this, but tugging round a slipped rug is not ideal, for it invariably pulls the hairs of the coat the wrong way and could lead to discomfort. If you are not riding you should still allow at least 5 minutes to take the rug off and re-set it, in which circumstance you can also check that it is not rubbing. Don't try to do this without first making sure you have control of the horse in the headcollar; trying to re-catch a horse in a dark, muddy field after he has run off with his rug half on and half off is no fun.

Weekend tasks

Generally speaking, the 'out' horse himself creates no more work for his owner at weekends than he does during the week, but there are still chores to be done if they have been neglected during the week. Water troughs need cleaning out about once a month; at a livery yard this task should be undertaken by the proprietors but in many cases it tends to be overlooked and falls to the clients. However, you can help keep the field water supply clean by taking a minute or so every other day to fish out any leaves that have dropped in; much of the 'gunge' that settles in the trough and taints the water results from these.

Management of the grazing again should fall to the yard proprietor at livery establishments. Major tasks like topping or harrowing are invariably contracted out by the single-horse owner in charge of his own grazing and disrupt only two or three weekend days a year. But those keeping horses on very small plots of land – say 2 acres or less – can also reap long-term benefits by spending, say, 30 minutes on Saturdays and Sundays removing piles of dung which otherwise reduce the amount of palatable grazing.

102

Your own clothes

If you are going straight to work from the yard you should allow at least 10 minutes to straighten yourself up for the office. The mark of well-planned horse-keeping is to arrive at work on time, looking as if you've come straight from home.

Some people try to save time by going to the yard half ready – i.e. with their working top on, only needing to replace jodhpurs and breeches with skirts or trousers. I am not sure this works, however, because if you have had a hard ride your clothes may well be hot and sweaty and never feel right for the day. However well protected, hay and other stable debris always seem to find their way on to sweaters, and so best clothes and horse clothes should remain firmly designated.

Sometimes if you have very few chores to do in the evening it is tempting just to throw a mac over your working clothes and to hurl on a pair of boots. Again, this can shorten the life of skirts and trousers, for one is inclined to forget that water and mud can still splash up on to them beneath the cover. Don't forget, too, that the wax can rub off unlined weatherproof jackets and coats and ruin a pale coloured garment beneath. I prefer to wear natural fibres but over the years have built up a wardrobe with a lot of synthetics for weekday use as they can take a lot more punishment of this nature without getting creased.

It may not look very horsy but the quickest and best protection for ordinary clothes is an inexpensive boiler suit; if big enough it can even go on over non-bulky skirts.

Gloves are a frequently overlooked solution to keeping hands clean; the commonly available cotton-knit riding gloves with plastic bobbled grips over the palms are also very good for working in and are so inexpensive that most people should be able to afford two or three pairs. Dirty fingernails and grimed-in dirt look horrible to the non-horseman; short fingernails and use of a heavy-duty industrial-type soap (like Swarfega) and barrier cream will help to keep these at bay. Always keep a pair of stout shoes that are easy to slip on and off readily available in your car or tack shed for last-minute dashes back into the yard if you remember something after you have changed for work; walking across uneven going or rummaging round a stable in decent shoes is the quickest way I know to write them off. Jewellery is out for riding, on grounds of etiquette and, more importantly, safety (getting a hooped ear-ring caught on a twig during a hack through a wood is extremely painful).

Hair can be a problem for those who ride before work. Riding hats, and especially non-ventilated crash skulls, invariably turn your hair into a sweaty, untidy mess. Unless you are so good at time-keeping that you can fit in a shower before you leave, all I can recommend is that the working rider opts for a simple hair style; if you run a comb through your hair within a few minutes of removing your hat you should be able to make it look acceptable before it dries into lifeless tresses that are impossible to rejuvenate during the day.

Those travelling reasonable distances by train can take advantage of this by changing on board in the public loos! A colleague of mine with an 80-mile trip into London on Inter-City used to do this and always looked immaculate, and, as she pointed out, she did not waste valuable 'horse' time at the yard. In any situation which involves transporting office clothes, cheap plastic suit covers supplied by dry cleaners are by far the most convenient way to carry such clothing without it getting grubby or creased in the car.

Chapter 10

Unexpected problems

The sick or injured horse

The horse in full work usually merits one day off per week – and obviously the owner will time this to coincide with his own busy schedule on weekdays. The trouble is that the working owner cannot afford to allow himself a bit of a lie-in on the mornings he does not ride. Murphy's Law says that the day you turn up late, allowing just enough time to do the stable work and turn out the horse before leaving for work, will be the day your horse has cut his legs to ribbons after getting cast during the night.

Generally speaking, most employers are sympathetic if you 'phone and explain that your horse has a serious problem that requires veterinary attention and which could cause you to be late at work, but it is a situation everyone should try to avoid. This is one very good reason why, if you elect to keep a horse on a DIY or part-DIY basis, you really must have someone to call on in times of emergency, whether it be a member of staff at the yard or just a willing, non-working friend.

There are numerous excellent books on horse ailments and veterinary matters and every owner should acquire the most up to date one possible, as well as keeping in touch with developments through articles in equestrian magazines. It is not my intention to go through an A to Z of first aid as this information is so readily available elsewhere. However, here are some thoughts on coping with the set-backs that most commonly affect working owners, who may hit a problem when no help is available, and for those with limited facilities.

One has to apply a degree of common sense, but there are very few circumstances in which you can apply a little first aid and dash off to work, leaving the vet to inspect the animal in your absence – even if they are old friends and the vet knows he won't kick or bite.

If you have a colic case you certainly can't leave the horse unattended because your priority, until professional help arrives, is to keep the animal on his feet. If the horse has a bad cut or wound that needs stitching, the vet will need you to assist by holding the horse while he completes this delicate task. And if you have a mysterious lameness, the vet can hardly be expected to make an accurate diagnosis if there is no one there to trot up the horse for him to spot the seat of the problem. Looking back, the only circumstance in which my own vets have been happy for me to 'leave them to it' has been when attending to respiratory problems in a horse where all other symptoms were normal.

So what should you do if you turn up and find an unexpected crisis with no one immediately available to help?

Pre-planning tends to be something busy horse-owners don't do enough of, even though it would make their lives so much easier. One thing you really must attend to, however, is the provision of a first-aid kit.

These can be bought ready-made but you can easily compile your own. It should include clean cotton-wool and Gamgee tissue, veterinary wound powder and antibiotic cream, a veterinary thermometer, a clean pair of scissors, at least two packets of Animalintex (a proprietary brand of poultice ideally suited to treatment of wounds and swellings), half a dozen packets of Melalin (an untreated fabric dressing that does not stick to the wound and which can usefully follow on from poulticing, to avoid the formation of proud flesh which can be associated with the latter), a Bonner or similarly chemically frozen bandage for first-aid treatment of suspected tendon injuries, Vetrap (a brand of stretchy bandage that has a semi-self-sticking quality and is thus easy to apply for the groom working with no help), clean stretch crêpe bandages, a needle and thread (for sewing up bandages – not for trying to stitch wounds yourself!), masking tape or other sticky tape that your vet may recommend, eye wash or drops, a bottle of Benylin expectorant (a cough mixture designed for humans and available at chemists but recommended by some vets as initial relief for stable coughs before professional help arrives), and some Clingfilm or similar self-sticking kitchen paper.

If you keep the horse away from home and do not have the use of a kitchen or other clean working area, you should keep a clean plate or plastic tray under wraps for preparing dressings such as Animalintex. If you do not have immediate access to clean running water (my nearest is 100 yards (metres) away – everyday drinking water comes out of a self-filling trough, clearly not clean enough for washing wounds), keep three or four used squeezy (plastic) bottles full of clean water in your tack shed or storage area. The contents can then be gently trickled over the wound to wash it out.

If you have no power to heat up a kettle you may well have to go home to fetch hot water for Animalintex dressings the night or morning the injury is discovered. Subsequently, you could take some to the yard from home in a vacuum flask and, in the evening, bring some from your place of work so that you do not have to travel out of your way.

Modern veterinary practice has no place for antiseptics or disinfectants, as it is now known that when administered direct on to wounds they can actually hamper if not kill the organisms promoting healing. However, it is wise to keep some on hand to disinfect any instruments, as first-aid kits kept in communal sheds do tend to get grubby and pick up dust.

If you keep your horse on isolated premises without a 'phone, keep an envelope in your first-aid kit with enough small change for the 'phone box (I can guarantee this will be a time when you don't have enough on you), and write the vet's surgery and after-hour's numbers on the front.

Whatever your vet advises, one thing common to horses laid-off through illness or injury is the need for round-the-clock supervision. If the working owner does not have formal assistance or kind friends or fellow liveries who will stand in, he may well have to negotiate an extra-long lunch-hour during a critical period so that he can return to the yard, even if only to give the patient a cursory glance, to change a dressing and skip out.

The sick horse will need checking at least four times a day, which may involve you in an extra late-night as well as lunchtime visit. If you have to administer drugs by injection (these days many vets will instruct responsible adults how to do this themselves when a straightforward course of antibiotics has to be administered intra-muscularly) you should try to lay on a succession of willing helpers. If experienced help is not available, then ask someone inexperienced to accompany you – not to help but to be there to raise the alarm if you get into difficulties.

With a sick horse, the working owner gains time by not having to ride; nor will the horse feel like being groomed or even led out in hand. But there will be extra responsibilities to take up the time. These will include keeping the stable and feed buckets perhaps more scrupulously clean than you have time for in normal circumstances, administering drugs, liaising with the veterinary surgeon and, most importantly, tempting the horse to eat. Thrown out of work, the horse normally needs his hard feed ration cut and hay fed *ad lib* to compensate, but the horse that feels really off-colour may be turned off by the monotony of 24-hour hay. The owner's responsibility is to whet his appetite: well-made bran mashes, freshly cut grass (though *not* lawn mowings – they ferment quickly and can cause colic), carefully chopped carrots and apples, and molasses can all help to perk him up.

The horse recovering from a bad cut or wound, however, will take rather more time-consuming management as he may be feeling quite bright in himself. As you cannot keep him entertained through the feed bowl because of his reduced concentrate ration you will have to use all your ingenuity to offset boredom, although, unlike the sick animal, he may enjoy being led out for exercise and to pick at grass for 20 minutes or so, three times a day, and grooming twice daily can break up his inactive day. The advantage of keeping a horse in a big yard, where there is plenty for him to watch, is obvious.

Although it creates extra work, I have found my stabled equine patients more likely to get stuck into the business of eating up their hay if I keep popping in with a fresh, small haynet, at lunchtime, rather than hanging up a whole day's worth first thing in the morning.

There have been occasions when, unable to get back at lunchtime, I have wrapped up my sound horse's injured leg like Fort Knox and risked turning him out for the day with a quiet friend to relieve boredom. I would not recommend it. However skilfully applied, on an active horse dressings always end up at half mast; you then not only expose the wound to dirt from the field but also risk further injury should the unravelled bandage get wound around another leg. Unless you have time to supervise, never turn out an injured horse before the wound is well on the way to recovery. As soon as your back is turned he will undo all your good work.

If you arrive at the field or yard after work and find cuts and wounds on your horse, the difficulty here is that you can have no idea how or when they were caused. If several hours old, dirt could already be well entrenched and infection set in. Another few minutes isn't going to make much difference to something that has stopped bleeding and formed a scab, so if it looks serious enough to require veterinary attention, call him straight away, then return to do what you can in the meanwhile. However, if the wound has not stopped bleeding of its own accord, you must apply a pressure bandage immediately and then call the vet without delay. If the wound is not on a limb but part of the trunk (thankfully a rare occurrence) there can be difficulty in securing the pressure pad; if you have assistance the spare pair of hands could literally hold the pad on while veterinary help is summoned. One time I had to do this single-handed and stuck the pad to the horse's coat with generous strips of masking tape. I knew this would not hold for long, as the blood and other moisture would dissolve the adhesive properties of the tape, but it served its purpose for the five minutes I had to spend on the 'phone.

Most of the wounds sustained in the field that do not need stitching are treated either by poulticing (usually with Animalintex) or by thorough washing out and dressing with lavish amounts of antibiotic or veterinary wound powder.

On the whole, deep or puncture wounds are usually poulticed to draw out the infection. Luckily, clear instructions for the use of Animalintex appears on the packet. For those struggling to apply the poultice and bandage it on single-handed, I have found that generous use of Clingfilm will hold the poultice firmly in place while you apply the bandage and will also help to keep the poultice in place during the long hours the horse goes without supervision, thereby fostering prompt recovery. (Before I was told this tip, I must have dropped dozens of poultices into the bedding when the horse inconsiderately moved!)

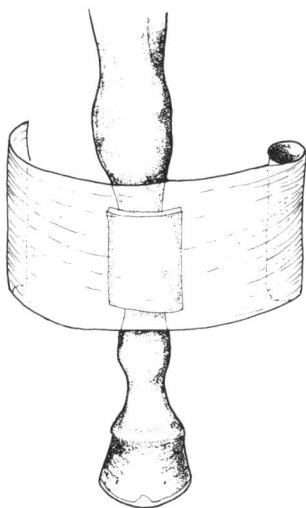

Use of Clingfilm or similar kitchen wrap to secure poultices when applying dressings single-handed (in conjunction with bandages).

109

Riding out and possible problems

Problems encountered while riding invariably account for more working owners turning up late at work than almost anything else. However meticulously you plan your morning exercise, a small hold-up, like running into an obstruction and having to take a different, longer route home, or something more serious, like falling off, can drastically throw out the rest of your pre-office timetable. So what can you do to minimise these eventualities?

Your riding should start quietly, and whether you are hacking or schooling you should stay in walk for the first 5 minutes to allow the horse to unwind, and also return to walk for the last ½ mile of your hack (or last 5-10 minutes of your time in the school) to enable the horse to relax and cool down. Everyone who rides is taught that patience is a virtue and that you should never lose your temper with an animal. I'm afraid that sometimes we all do, but from bitter experience I would urge you not to pick a fight with your horse, however much you feel provoked, when pushed for time, and especially not within 20 minutes of the end of your riding period. The upshot of such 'scenes' is usually a distressed, sweaty horse.

If he doesn't solve the immediate problem or 'win' the argument the considerate full-time rider has the option of calming the horse down and drying him off by taking him for a relaxing hack. The working owner does not have the luxury of this time and in rushing a hot horse back to the yard to complete the morning's chores he can compromise the animal's health in three ways.

First, it is as foolhardy to hard feed a horse on top of strenuous exercise as it is to exercise a horse on top of a full feed. The pulse rate and breathing in a distressed horse remain high for a considerable period; the more obvious repercussion of feeding a horse before his recovery is complete is that you could cause him to choke – a frightening experience and one that is impossible to cope with on your own. The second problem is that if the blood supply is being taxed to help the vital organs recover, it detracts from the performance of the digestive juices. (With time on your side, in such a situation, I would wait at least 30 minutes before offering feed.) The third problem is that a sweaty horse needs careful drying off – and the person trying to rush away from the yard may be tempted to skimp this, opening the horse to the risk of chills, whether in the stable or out.

110

You should, of course, make every effort to ensure this eventuality never arises, but if your horse does get hot there are various ways of handling it. None of them is ideal and it is a case of picking the lesser of the evils, depending on the amenities at your disposal and whether you have back-up assistance to complete the task after you have left for work.

In warm, sunny weather the horse damp with sweat is probably best turned straight out in the field where he will have a roll, which not only helps to dry the coat but also, and more importantly, makes him relax and therefore reduces the risk of him breaking-out with sweat again. Unless he has company, he could either have his breakfast later in the field, or be brought in if help is available. In this case recovery should be straightforward. In typical spring and autumn weather the damp but not dripping horse can go straight out with his usual New Zealand rug on if you have no help and have to leave for work. But if it is bitterly cold or very wet and windy I would recommend keeping him in with an anti-sweat rug under his usual stable wear as the risk of chills is too great. The horse standing in should have a haynet to pick at and can be given his breakfast later when he has cooled off. If you have to feed straight away, offer just a 'token' breakfast and make up for the reduced quantity over the course of the feeds given during the next 24 hours.

If the horse is saturated with sweat, in all but very cold weather the best thing is to give him a complete wash down, which will take 5-10 minutes, using lukewarm water and thoroughly scraping the water away. The method you choose to dry him depends again on the availability of help to finish off the job if you have to leave promptly. He can be left in his box, suitably rugged, with a haynet, in which circumstance you will be obliged to return to him at lunchtime, or be dried off by the traditional method of 'thatching' (stuffing a lining of straw across his back under his rugs or sheet). An infra-red lamp is a now common piece of equipment in many yards but use of this to dry your horse is only convenient for the working owner if someone else is around to rug up your horse when he has dried and to return him to his box or field.

Washing horses is a relatively new practice; in the past it used to be frowned upon because it was said to remove too much natural grease from the coat, causing chills; and it was generally thought of as a lazy method of horse care. These days, however, authoritative horse-keepers have disproved the theory where stabled horses are concerned, although one should add that the horse living out

111

full-time, or the horse going out during the day without clothing, should not be washed.

In the past, the practice for coping with a hot horse would be to allow the sweat to dry and then brush it off later. However, this can be a very time-consuming task and if done only half-heartedly, waste matter and body salts can be rubbed back into the skin when the horse is next ridden and can contribute to sores and galls.

The other related problem that can upset your morning timetable is getting caught out in unexpected rain and arriving back at the yard with an animal soaking wet from a downpour. Again, the slightly damp horse can be turned out with his rug on with reasonable safety in all but very cold, windy weather, but the saturated animal will have to be handled as above. The problem can be avoided by judicious selection of waterproof rugs. Rain sheets and quarter sheets take a few extra minutes to put on and sometimes, if the weather looks dubious, it can be tempting to risk it and go without them. On the other hand, if you take waterproofs with you (lightweight versions can be easily rolled up and tied to the saddle or carried in a 'bum bag'), you may have to stop to put them on in less than ideal circumstances and the horse could already be soaked before you complete the task. The ingenious solution is to invest in one of the combined horse and rider capes, which cover the rider, and his legs (and therefore the horse's trunk all round the saddle area), and stretch over the horse's back and loins. The advantages are that you don't have to get off, as you would if you had to fit a conventional rain sheet, and the cape is less likely to twist or slip round the horse than the former. I would, however, most strongly recommend that the rider has a few practice runs at putting on such a cape while mounted in controlled conditions at home before surprising the horse with a huge flapping 'dragon' out on the hack.

Lost shoes

If your horse's shoes are remotely loose you should not venture far on your hacks and it may be prudent to stay at 'base' and ride in the school, if available, until the blacksmith has been. However, very occasionally the horse will unexpectedly pull off a shoe when you are out on a hack. You should immediately turn back for home, get off and lead the horse and show every possible consideration to your animal. It is only really permissible to continue riding him if the going is soft all the way and, even then, trot only if you really

Riding out in a combined cape/rain sheet, easy to put on when caught out in rain on exercise.

have to. This is because, unlike the animal that is permanently unshod, the feet of the shod animal never get the chance to harden off and, in addition, the stress exerted to pull off a shoe is also usually enough to take off some of the wall of the hoof, which makes contact with a hard or rough surface painful and the source of further damage. Unfortunately one does not always notice a lost shoe when riding out, and as the hind feet tend to have more resilience than the forefeet, the horse may not show signs of 'footiness' or lameness straight away. I still cringe to think of the time this happened to me on a cross-country school: by the time we'd finished and noticed the trouble, so much of the foot had broken away that my farrier nearly refused to try to put on a new shoe on grounds of cruelty!

Such problems can be avoided if the farrier visits regularly, so that the fitting of the shoes never reaches the 'hanging on by a thread' state. This is easier said than done, for working owners not based in a yard where a visiting farrier is one of the perks, invariably have great difficulty getting a farrier to attend during the owner's limited spare time, although it has to be said that these days farriers are inclined to work at weekends.

Another problem is that horses being only lightly ridden, or worked mainly on manège surfaces, have rarely worn out their

113

shoes when re-shoeing is theoretically due, and there is a strong temptation to try to make them last a couple more weeks. This is bad horsemanship, however, for if the foot is allowed to grow too long it forces the horse on to his heels and in turn upsets the relationship and function of the joints of the lower leg, which can lead to all sorts of locomotive problems. In its extreme form, letting the foot grow too long is rather like getting a cobbler to tap small platforms on to the front of a human's shoes and then asking the wearer to try walking properly in them! Frankly, the only reliable (and possibly more costly) solution is to make a regular four or five-weekly booking with your farrier for the first call in the morning, and stick to it whether the horse actually needs him or not. This way you will not have to keep chasing the farrier on the 'phone from the office when you have a crisis; nor will you waste untold days of your annual holiday leave hanging around for a farrier who said he'd be with you 'early afternoon' but who got held up by a previous client and does not in fact surface until half past five. . .

Chapter 11

Safety

The first thing anyone is taught when he or she first begins an association with a horse is that, even in its domesticated state, it is a nervy, sensitive creature that takes fright easily, often irrationally, and has lightening-quick reactions which make it want to flee from potential danger.

To cope with this the horseman is encouraged to be firm but quiet at all times, to keep his temper, however severe the provocation (it is pointless to have a fight, because even if you feel some satisfaction after a 'scene' with your animal, the horse really doesn't understand the concept of 'scoring points' over people), and to avoid any loud noises or sudden movements that may panic the animal.

Sadly, however early the working owner gets up, and however diligently he has prepared his timetable, he does not always have time to do tasks in the correct but methodical fashion. It only needs some small delay – like the necessary treatment of a minor abrasion sustained on the ride, or the need to dry off a horse that got caught unexpectedly in a shower – to throw out the rest of the morning's plans. The frequent result is that the owner, desperately trying to make up time, ends up rushing round his horse in the box. Not understanding the owner's sudden agitation, the horse can get upset and confused, maybe failing to react to commands as he would normally do. Tempers get more frayed and it is in these situations that the risk of stable accidents is just round the corner.

Tying up

A great many accidents result from lack of control of the horse in the box, and these in turn from failing to tie up the horse due to the simple lack of the right stable fittings. There is a school of thought that you should have as few fittings in the box as possible, and indeed there is wisdom in this as horses have a strange tendency to injure themselves on the most insignificant projections. But to become efficient, the working owner really should get in the habit of tying up his horse for the duration of his early morning, pre-work visits. The horse that moves about the box while you are trying to work is not only hazardous but, by getting in the way, literally doubles the time you take per task. Stable fittings ideally include two tying-up rings, one in the middle of the wall (to which the haynet is usually attached), and one maybe in the corner, ideally where the horse eats his hard feed. Some traditionalists dislike corner mangers or other kinds of receptacles (such as door mangers) that oblige the horse to eat from a unnatural, chest height. Nonetheless, unless you have a specific reason to feed the horse off the ground (veterinary surgeons may recommend it to help give relief to horses with, for instance, nasal discharges), I would advise anyone who has to work in the stable while the horse eats, to feed him from the corner manger on weekday mornings at least. This means that the horse can be tied up and left to eat his feed, getting him right out of your hair while you complete mucking out, changing the water buckets or other chores. It may seem remarkably petty but I can guarantee it saves time and irritation. (For safety's sake, corner mangers should be blocked in underneath, so that the horse does not get stuck under it if cast.)

Tying up is a skill that has to be learned. While one wants control, sometimes in a panic situation you will have to release the horse from his tenure; the frightened horse instinctively pulls back from any restraint. (Inexperienced horse-keepers commonly underestimate the strength of the horse, and this is often apparent by looking at the sort of fixtures to which people with inadequate facilities will tie their horses. I have seen a horse pull off a car bumper at least three times over the years!) For this you must master the quick-release knot illustrated. Some headcollar ropes and leading reins have a quick-release mechanism where they clip on to the headcollar. They should still be used in conjunction with a quick-release knot should the mechanism jam. Also on grounds of safety, the horse should not be secured direct to the wall-mounted ring; tie a small loop of baling twine to the ring and then tie the rope to this for two reasons. First, the twine will stand up to a fair amount of strain but in real emergencies will give way, and thus spare the horse further panic-making distress from the pressure on his headcollar, and even the possibility that he could pull the

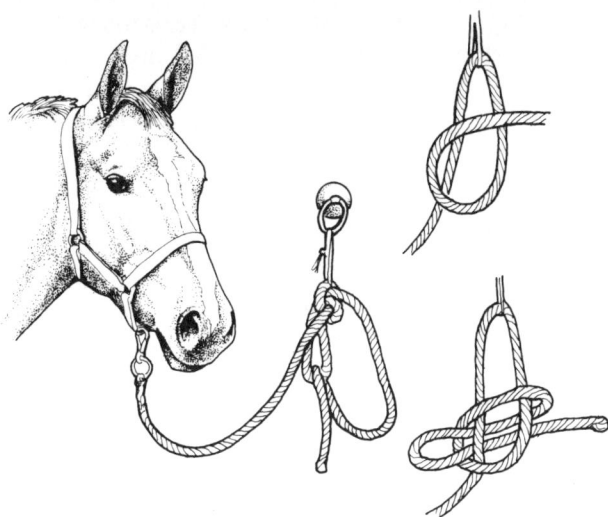

The correct way to tie a quick-release knot. Note the use of a loop of binder twine between the rope and tying-up ring as an additional safety precaution.

ring out of the wall. Second, as the twine takes the initial strain of a sudden pull or jerk, the handler has a chance to get to the quick-release knot before it too is pulled into a tight knot that no one can disentangle. Never allow a long loop of the rope to dangle, as the unattended horse could get his leg caught over it; again this could cause him to panic, for the horse does not have the sense of logic that tells him to wait quietly for assistance.

Somewhat out of fashion these days, though still of value, is the log and ball system, still used where horses are kept permanently tied up in stalls. Here the rope is threaded through a grapefruit-sized wooden ball, secured by a quick-release knot for safety's sake. The other end is passed through a wall-mounted ring and attached to the headcollar in the normal way. With this device, the horse has greater freedom while still being under control in the box and does not risk getting his leg caught over the rope as the slack is automatically taken up by the weight of the log.

In conjunction with tying up, all horses should be taught to stand still at the back of the box and to move from side to side when instructed. It is not difficult; no horse is too old to learn and all it needs is quiet determination – you do not want to terrorise the horse into a frightened wreck cowering at the back when you appear – and persistence – in my experience, most people give up

117

trying if they have no success after three days. Some horses get so disciplined that they do not have to be tied up in the end, which is a useful time-saver for busy owners, but even if this happy situation arises, never ever let the horse get between you and an open door.

Sometimes horses and ponies have to be tied up in the field. The most common occasions are when they are being given hard feed – it is extremely difficult to persuade loose animals to stick to their own bowls. But often it is simply for grooming or tacking-up when grass livery owners have no option other than to prepare their horses in the field. Whatever the reason, and even when under constant supervision, loose horses should not be allowed to wander amongst the tied-up animals for obvious safety reasons.

Always tie the horse, via the baling twine loop, to the upright posts along the fence line, never the horizontal rails or cross-members of the gate as again the horse has the strength to take these with him if he panics and pulls away. If tying up in the field is a regular thing, one should consider fitting proper tying-up rings to the uprights. It is safer to feed a tied-up horse from a door manger hooked over the gate rather than from a bucket on the ground, as there can be a temptation to tie the rope to a spot too low on the fence so that the horse can reach the feed bowl easily; this is a dangerous practice for, again if he panics, the sudden downward pull can be enough to break his neck.

Horses can, of course, be fed loose in the field but this only works if all the animals know their 'pecking order' and can be trusted to stick to their own meals. To prevent waste you can sit the buckets or bowls in old car tyres, which prevents the enthusiastic feeder from overturning them. Buckets should not be left in the field when not in use because of the risk of the horse cracking the plastic and putting his leg right through the bottom (a particular hazard in very cold weather when some plastics are liable to shatter). If you feed from buckets, remove the handle first as, if the bucket tips over, this is another thing the horse can put his foot through.

Waiting to go out

Once tacked up, if the horse is not being taken out of his box immediately he can either be tied up or left untied but with the reins twisted and threaded through the throatlatch as shown, safely out of harm's way. This traditional method, being marginally more fiddly, tends to be overlooked by those with one eye on the clock. But however rushed you are, always tie up a bridled horse via a headcollar put on over the bridle, even if it is going to be for a couple of minutes. Never tie up by the reins, or by clipping a lead rope to the bit, for if the horse should pull back he will frighten himself even more by hurting his mouth and could also break the bridle.

Another malpractice frequently seen amongst riders in a hurry is leaving the horse tacked up and popping out of the stable 'just for a couple of seconds' – to fetch, perhaps, a hat or stick – leaving the door closed but not bolted. The horse only needs a couple of seconds to wander over to the door; he can so easily push the door slightly ajar and catch the reins over the top corner. If he then pulls back he shuts the door on himself and can not only panic himself witless but also break the bridle or even pull the door inwards against the hinges. Unfortunately, in this situation, which results entirely from sloppiness, the owner can only stand by and watch helplessly until something breaks.

If you get into the habit of always bolting the door, top and bottom, when you go in and out you should avoid the situation

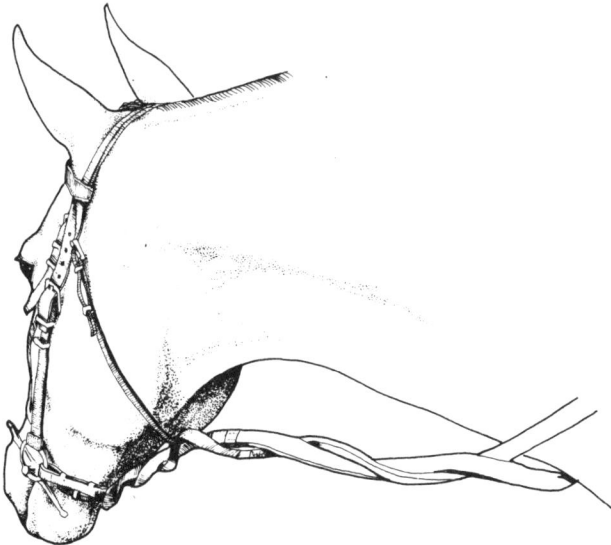

A horse can be more safely left tacked up in his stable for a few moments with the reins twisted and secured through the throatlatch; this prevents them slipping forward over his head.

119

of setting off for work or home and having to turn back when it suddenly occurs to you that you may not have secured the door.

The price of leather headcollars has meant that, for normal stable use, nylon has taken over. Such synthetic headcollars can be thrown in the wash, last for years and, because they can be inexpensively replaced, it is not such an inconvenience if they get lost or permanently 'borrowed' by others in large communal yards. However, for the very reason that nylon rarely breaks, such headcollars should not be left on a horse in the field in case he gets caught up on the fence or the branch of a tree. If your horse is hard to catch and you have to keep something on him, secondhand leather that no one would want for 'Sunday best' can be bought inexpensively and will do for the field.

Foreign bodies

As mentioned earlier, horses have an alarming tendency to damage themselves on minor projections in their stables. Therefore it follows that any foreign bodies left in the box, however momentarily, constitute a hazard. These might include mucking-out tools, items from the grooming kit, unrolled bandages or headcollars dangling from the tying-up ring. Removing these items is something that people in a hurry are inclined to forget. Sadly, you really cannot trust a horse not to get into mischief while your back is turned! I have a spare door manger which I hook over the door during stable work and this can be used to keep small items in frequent use off the floor and out of harm's way when I am dashing back and forth. Some grooming kit boxes sold commercially have elasticated fabric covers which are usually the right size to slip over the door manger and thus prevent curious, untied animals from investigating the contents.

The stabled horse is also at risk from mucking-out tools while they are being used. Although it is often done, it is extremely dangerous to fork and dig out bedding around your horse's feet and legs. You may think he is placid and too interested in his feed to notice you, but he only has to lift his leg against an imaginary fly to catch himself on the prongs. Here, again, it is important to keep the horse tied up and sufficiently disciplined to be moved round the box and out of the way on command.

The busy owner must discipline himself to take the time and trouble to keep the stable hazard-free at all times. In the long term it will pay dividends.

Riding out

Every day there are eight accidents on the road involving horses, according to the British Horse Society's road safety office, which is the first to admit the estimate is low. The failure of the Department of Transport to recognise the problems and requirements of horses on the road has not helped the accurate compilation of statistics, nor the spread of information to the 'lay public' about how to react to a horse on the road. With an increase in both cars and horses on the road, the number of accidents – and fatalities – must be going up.

The BHS runs riding and road safety tests and the newcomer is strongly recommended to study the requirements and observe them in his daily riding, even if he or she does not put himself forward for the test. In any event, you should not venture out on the road unless you have a horse that is reliable in traffic and until you are crystal clear about the Highway Code as it applies to horses.

There are certain aspects of particular relevance to the working owner-rider, and so we will examine them in detail here.

Whereas it is absolutely true that a great number of traffic incidents result from either the ignorance, impatience or plain bloody-mindedness of the vehicle driver, it has to be said that riders often fail to play their part in accident prevention. I am not just talking about sensible riding, or having the good manners to thank drivers who have slowed down for you, but simply by neglecting to give drivers ample warning that you are there. In this respect, traditional riding wear made out of muted, green-brown tweeds, or the more modern olive-coloured waxed jackets are not ideal to wear when riding on the roads because they act as camouflage against the hedgerows when instead the rider should be as obvious as a belisha beacon! This point was well made at a seminar on safety I attended a few years ago, when medical researchers showed a video of an experiment along these lines. An experienced rider wearing traditional garb rode up and down a busy stretch of road where the reaction time and passing speed of every car that went by in either direction was recorded. Next day, in identical weather conditions and at the same time, the rider went along the same stretch of road wearing a fluorescent safety tabard, and with her horse sporting fluorescent legstraps. The speed of most passing cars dropped and the vast majority reacted to the sight of the horse at about twice the distance away. Your priority therefore is to be seen; it is not 'cissy' to wear a bright green or orange safety

121

tabard and hat cover, but if you can't bear it one of the fashionable brightly coloured quilted riding coats will make an adequate substitute.

The working owner is particularly at risk on the roads because he has to ride either early in the morning or after work. At all times of year he is therefore out on the roads when the traffic is at its heaviest and, of course, in winter he has the extra problem of poor light. In all cases he should dress as visibly as possible, equip his horse with safety boots or leg straps and strongly consider investing in a stirrup light. This is worn on the rider's offside (right), and therefore towards the traffic, with the red light to the rear. If riding in a party, the leader should have a single white light to the front and the last rider a red light only, showing to the rear. These two riders should keep their places in the line at all times, otherwise in half-light, vehicle drivers will be confused.

Ride and lead

Ride and lead offers the obvious time-saving alternative of being able to exercise two horses at once. For working owners with more than one horse it is usually an essential skill, although friends may take turns to take out each other's horses while the other stays behind to do two lots of stable work to maximise the amount of exercise a horse has on each office day.

Ride and lead is not as daunting as it sounds but, like everything else to do with horses, certain ground rules have to be observed for safety's sake.

First, the two horses should be as well mannered as possible and known to get on with each other. In theory you should swap them each day so that one horse does not go a whole week without a saddle on its back, but if the horses show a marked preference for being the leader or the led I would recommend sticking to it rather than risking a problem.

The led horse should always wear a bridle, as the rider will not have sufficient control off a headcollar only. He can be led by the reins, taken over his head, or from a cotton (not nylon – it can burn the skin if pulled) lunge rein. The latter gives the leader a longer length to play with in an emergency, but this longer length should not tempt the rider to let the led horse dawdle or get behind the ridden animal; as soon as this happens one loses control. The led animal should always be to the near-side (left), so that the ridden animal, correctly going in the same direction as the traffic, not

122

Horse and rider correctly attired for ride and lead. The led horse is bridled for extra control and led from the near-side, i.e. away from the traffic.

against it as would a pedestrian, effectively forms a controllable 'buffer' between him and the traffic. The led horse should be made to keep his position so that his head is level with the rider's knee.

It should go without saying that the rider should practice ride and lead in controlled conditions, like the manège or paddock, before going out on roads or open spaces and should plan his route carefully to avoid possible hazards like roadworks.

Finding a left-handed circuit round the lanes when first embarking on ride and lead will help as the led horse is always being turned to the inside at junctions, rather than being dragged to the outside across the traffic as he would at right-handed junctions. Try to avoid rural routes with particularly narrow lanes and blind bends because of your extra width. Having said that, however, I have frequently found drivers far more considerate towards horses being ridden and led rather than two being ridden abreast, though I expect they slow down because of the novelty value rather than because of understanding of the rider's problems.

Ride and lead should always be viewed primarily as a means of exercise. I strongly advise against trying to combine it with school-ing, however frustrating you find this wasted opportunity. By this I mean the use of side-reins, running reins or other gadgets that are aimed at keeping either horse in some sort of outline. Whereas it can also be argued that a semi-restrained animal is less likely to get away from the leader, I feel that the presence of extra reins and straps at chest level is extremely hazardous; there is the risk that horses and rider can get their legs tangled up in all this extra 'knitting'. For the same reason one should not attempt to secure one horse to another via the tack.

Chapter 12

Winter

A spell of snow and freezing weather never fails to catch Britain by surprise. But for the working horse owner it can become a particular nightmare as the already time-consuming task of horse-keeping becomes even more demanding and the difficulties of travelling on frozen roads can mean there is even less time than usual to spend at the stables.

Do not panic; those who rush about are quite likely to slip over and may even break an arm or a leg, making themselves useless to both their horse and their boss. Take your time and try not to worry about keeping to a schedule. Most employers are sympathetic in very bad weather, and owners who just keep going quietly will probably find that they get to work at the same time as usual.

In difficult circumstances it is often the obvious which is overlooked. Here are some reminders to make life easier and safer and to help keep your horse in such condition that he can be brought back into work as swiftly as possible after an enforced lay off.

Horses at grass

Whatever the weather, a constant supply of water is required by the horse. Unfortunately, strong as the horse is, he is ill-equipped to break through even a thin layer of ice over his water supply, so this task has to be done for him daily. Most people remember to crack the ice on the trough in the morning but forget that in really cold weather it will freeze over again during the day and need a second attack in the evening. If your horses are on the spot it cannot hurt to give the trough another go before you go to bed, too.

One should never wait for the weather to get so bad that it freezes all the external pipes. They should be insulated as soon as the weather forecasters predict a cold snap. There is no need to buy proper insulating materials if you cannot afford them; empty feed sacks can be thickly bundled round pipes and secured with baling twine with very good results.

If you fill troughs with a hose-pipe, take the trouble to disconnect and drain it each night, and store it somewhere warm or under cover. This takes considerably less time than having to de-freeze a hose left out in the field overnight.

Horses and ponies living out will already be receiving hay to supplement the poor nutritive value of grazing available in the winter. They will easily withstand a spell of snow and freezing weather as long as it remains dry and the wind is not strong, and provided the hay ration is further increased to make up for the bulk they miss in the grass they cannot reach. It is when the thaw sets in that horses can lose condition. This is partly because they find it harder to withstand persistent wet conditions than cold, dry weather, and partly because owners tend to think that the worst is over and reduce the hay ration. Extra hay is, in fact, needed more than ever as the snow will have made the grass shrivelled and unappetising.

The hay should be put out in the part of the field where the animals are inclined to spend most of their time sheltering from the elements (which in freezing conditions may not necessarily be their usual haunt). Make sure there are more piles than horses and ponies so that the weaker ponies do not lose out to the bullies.

If hay is fed *ad lib* then the provision of extra hard feed is up to the individual. Although one should, in theory, reduce hard feed drastically if the horse is thrown out of work, obviously in very cold weather he will still need some to provide energy to maintain his body temperature. If the horse seems to get by on one feed a day it is still preferable to split it into two or three feeds if practicable because of the comforting effect; we all know how much warmer we feel with even a small meal in our stomach. Extra hard feed will probably be a necessity for young and old horses and ponies.

If the horses are good doers it may be more practicable to supply a keep block for the animals to nibble at their leisure to obtain minerals and vitamins, rather than hard feeding more than once a day. For owners pushed for time this is probably preferable to leaving buckets and feed bowls lying in the fields, as plastics are likely to shatter in freezing weather and horses can put their feet right through them – a recipe for disaster.

Unshod animals will need special supervision as hard, rutty ground can split the wall of the hoof and cause bruised soles and heels. All should have their feet picked out night and morning;

compacted snow can expand and freeze round the sole with uncomfortable results. New Zealand rugs will, of course, need re-fitting daily as usual, for even the best may slide back or round to one side.

Never worry about appearing to be a busy-body if you spot a neighbour's or fellow livery owner's horse that does not seem to have moved; it is not unknown for cold or poor horses to get frozen to the spot in very severe weather.

Stabled horses

Owners lucky enough to have the use of indoor schools should be able to give their horses a reasonable work/exercise programme. But those whose horses are going to be completely box-bound by the snow, or who can only get out for a cautious walk around the edge of the field, will need to adopt a completely different routine for the fit stabled horse if 'tying up' or a host of temperamental problems are to be avoided.

Some horses are naturally disposed towards tying up but, as previously described, it commonly results from a period of rest with no corresponding reduction of hard feed. The safest way is to rug up well, cut out hard feed completely, or at least reduce it to a token feed, and put the stabled horse on to *ad lib* hay, which will also help to relieve boredom in a horse who would normally expect to be ridden and turned out for the greater part of the day. Epsom salts in the drinking water and, once the horse comes back into work gradually, a vitamin E supplement (preferably one containing selenium, the enzyme which uses the vitamin) will help to keep the azoturia threat at bay. In bad weather there is a temptation to give a box-bound horse an extra scoop of nuts to cheer him up, but this is a grave mistake. If you want to give him a treat, stick to carrots.

Automatic waterers are likely to freeze at an early stage so the busy owner who usually relies on them will have to allow extra time to fill buckets from a tap – and this may often involve a long trip from a kitchen if the outside pipes have also seized up.

Insulated water buckets are available; they are expensive but may provide the solution for the owner who can only get to his horse before and after work. A clean rubber or plastic ball can be floated in a water bucket to delay the freezing process but there is no failsafe way to stop ice forming across the top other than by regular cracking. As everyone knows, salt stops water freezing but please don't add it to your buckets; the amount needed would make the drink unpalatable!

126

Extra warmth is best provided in the long-term by additional rugs rather than greatly increased quantities of hard feed. If you run out of conventional rugs, blankets and quilted underclothes, don't forget that thin layers – such as summer sheets – will also trap warm air. Duvet seconds, bought cheaply from market stalls, have also been used successfully by enterprising owners.

When putting on three or four rugs at a time, place them on the horse allowing plenty of room at the chest and then pull the lot back into place as one unit. If you fit each rug individually the one nearest the coat will be yanked further back as successive layers are applied and by the time the top rug is fastened the bottom one will be throttling its unfortunate wearer. According to traditional stable practice, one neatly folds blankets back under the roller. In cold weather I let them cover the neck (as would a neck cover on a New Zealand rug); the more of the horse you keep covered up, the warmer he will be. Likewise, stable bandages provide extra warmth by heating more of the horse's extremities and encouraging good circulation, but if you have not got time to reapply them night and morning I would recommend forgetting them altogether. Bandages that slip and pinch curtail the circulation instead of assisting it and can even damage tendons.

As discussed in a previous chapter I would not recommend deep-litter bedding as a general rule, but there is a case for it in very bad weather. Firstly, from the point of view of the horse, it provides valuable warmth. Secondly, from the practical viewpoint of the busy owner, it reduces the amount of muck you have to empty during a period when it may be unduly difficult and time-consuming to get to the muck-heap. However, because deep-litter bedding does foster the fungal spores that cause respiratory disorders it is best not to resort to it if your horse is remotely suspect in his wind; and, of course, it all has to be dug out in the end.

Whether you use deep litter or stick to conventional bedding management, horses normally clean in the wind may start to cough a little if confined to the box all day. The answer would normally be to soak hay but as cold, ice-encrusted haynets are no fun for horse or handler alike, this may not be practicable unless you can move the trough or soaking bin into a heated utility room or similar. Steaming offers an alternative; the haynet can be ready within the hour, although, as previously discussed, steamed hay does make some horses loose in their droppings. Sugar-beet should also be brought into the house or other warm area to be soaked, but if this means you have to take dry pulp nuts home in the back of your car, remember to use a bucket with a lid for the return journey. Pouring boiling water over frozen sugar-beet in the morning may make it more appetising but one should be aware that the water may have solidified in the cold before the sugar-beet had properly swelled the night before, and you could therefore be inadvertently giving indigestible feed to the horse.

In bad weather the decision whether to ride the stabled horse, turn it out, or both, depends entirely on the facilities available to the owner – some livery yards may impose a complete ban on turn-out, so you have no choice – the conditions underfoot and the temperament of the horse. If your only option is to ride on narrow, twisty roads with poor visibility or that have not been cleared or gritted, I would strongly urge staying in and resigning yourself to keeping the horse happy by diligent stable management. In the mornings before work, car drivers will be concentrating on bad road conditions and will probably find it hard to believe that anyone would be potty enough to want to ride in the snow. Your horse's well-being is important but riding out on public highways in snow is inconsiderate to other road-users. What is more, the best behaved, most footsure horse is the world is not going to escape injury if a passing car skids out of control.

Horses who normally enjoy being turned out all day usually get fed up after an hour playing in the snow and want to come in. As soon as they start to wait at the gate they get cold. This aspect undoubtedly causes the most severe disruption to the working owner's routine, as unless he has a mid-morning coffee break and can nip back to the stables he cannot get the horse in without help. There is no doubt that some sort of break out of the stable first thing puts the horse in a good frame of mind and encourages him to settle down for the rest of the day and get on with the business of tucking into his hay. When unable to ride, I have always found that allowing the horse a mere 15- or 20-minute frolic round the paddock while I do the mucking out has satisfied my animals. I usually put a New Zealand rug straight over the stable rugs. This, of course, saves loads of time but my motives are not entirely lazy; if you remove the stable rugs to put on the New Zealand you throw away the warm air pocket and end up putting cold rugs on again when the horse comes in a quarter of an hour or so later, so the heating up process has to start all over again. During long periods of bad weather and restricted riding I also usually turn the horses out for 10-15 minutes after work in the dark if an adjacent paddock is available, because they do seem to appreciate a quick mooch about and again will tuck into the haynet supplied for the long night ahead with more enthusiasm on their return. The two things to watch are, first, to brush off any snow stuck to the rugs before it melts and dampens the clothing; and second, when re-fitting the rugs do so by pulling them forward and then back again in the direction of the horse's coat to the required spot. This disturbs the warm air pockets as little as possible.

If you have a safe outdoor place to ride, remember to lubricate the horse's soles with hoof oil, cod liver oil or one of the sprays now commercially available to prevent snow gathering in the foot and 'balling'. This can make movement difficult if not downright dangerous as the foot is forced to an unnatural angle – rather like suddenly being shod with stiletto heels. Take a hoof-pick with you in case your lubrication wears off.

If you are going out for more than 20 minutes and doubt that you will get out of walk, use an exercise blanket as even unclipped animals suddenly exposed to the elements will get cold. The traditional golden-striped blanket has the advantage of making you more visible from a distance on the roads. If you do not usually use leg protectors I would recommend booting or bandaging in snow to reduce the risk of injuries if the horse should slip: but beware, some bandages are inclined to slip down to half-mast when damp.

If you are stuck for safe going but are fortunate enough to keep your horse in a quadrangled yard with others, you can all 'muck-in' and create a circular non-slip surface by mucking straight out of the door. It will, of course, be a chore to remove in the thaw but gives something round which the horses can at least be led.

Most horse-owners are fresh-air fans and keep the top doors open at all times. However, tune in regularly to weather forecasts and if a blizzard seems possible either during the day when you are at work or during the night shut it up – though only, of course, if the box has adequate ventilation. Remove icicles from guttering or any prominent fixtures; such projections have been known to break off and pierce the skin.

Keep an eye on your tack, too; leather stored in sub-zero temperatures can split and crack, the danger of which is obvious. If your tack shed is not well insulated then take these items home during the cold snap.

Last of all, look after yourself; don't empty water buckets where it may freeze and cause treacherous going for yourself and others; and invest if you can in 'high-tech' thermal gloves and socks. Riders with numb hands and feet cannot be in full control.

Chapter 13

Insurance and security

Insurance is full of complexities for any horse-keeper. Some people talk of such difficulties in trying to get an insurance company to settle a claim that the first-time horse-keeper may sometimes wonder if taking out any sort of cover is really worth the trouble. Properly-thought-out horse insurance is worth it and a great safeguard and reassurance to anyone unable to keep their horses at home or under the full-time supervision they would prefer. The accent is, however, very much on the properly-thought-out as in many circumstances, especially for those with horses of low value, the complete package deals generally on offer are not always cost-effective, as we shall see later. New horse-keepers may note that inexpensive membership of the British Horse Society and the British Show Jumping Association offers automatic third-party cover, which is essential for all. Some brokers offer specialist cover for veterinary fees only and together these two arrangements may be enough to satisfy most normal risks. Whether obtained through BHS or BSJA membership or through an insurance company, you should note that third-party cover only usually applies to your legal liability for a damages claim, not moral liability; so if, as happened to me, your horses escape and run amok over the well-tended lawns of the local manor house, you will not necessarily get any help towards reinstating the damaged turf.

However, insurance is based on two-way trust. You have every right to expect a company to honour a *bona fide* claim promptly, but at the same time it is wrong to trick the insurer into accepting a horse whose current condition or history suggests he is an unreasonable risk, on the same terms and premiums as those for a horse fit and healthy at the time the policy was taken out. Readers of the magazine I work for often 'phone us for advice over difficult claims and I am sorry to say that in many cases the company has been justified, technically if not always morally, in refusing to settle.

130

Often these cases have resulted from the policy-holders' failure to read the 'small print' carefully the moment they have received the policy document, as a result of which they have misunderstood exactly how far the cover will go. Sometimes problems simply arise from procedural shortcomings – the owner does not notify the insurance company immediately there is an incident which could result in a claim, and when he finally gets round to it months later the insurance company declines to help as it is almost impossible to determine the sequence of events. Insurance companies are in business to make money and will as a matter of course look for loopholes that may invalidate a claim; the art is for the policy-holder to keep one step ahead, anticipate these loopholes and clear them up in writing before an incident arises that could result in a claim.

In many more cases, the policy-holder pays the price of failing to disclose pre-existing conditions or soundness problems that he knows the horse already has, however harmless they may appear, at the time he took out the policy.

For example, a rider buys a horse with a known dust allergy which does not affect his everyday work but has to be managed to ward off more serious respiratory problems. He takes out insurance but fails to disclose the allergy. Some time later the horse gets a bad cough related to a chest infection which requires veterinary treatment and a long period off work. The owner claims on his policy for reimbursement of veterinary fees, but when the vet is asked by the insurer to submit a report to them about the case he notes that the horse already has a 'wind' problem. The company thus refuses to settle the claim because they had not been informed that the horse was more susceptible than normal to respiratory problems.

Another bone of contention often relates to the purpose for which is the horse is used. To determine premiums, insurance companies usually classify equestrian activities in order of risk. The least risk is attached to hacking, dressage and show jumping, working up the scale through hunting, hunter trials and eventing, and drag-hunting to steeplechasing, the greatest risk of all and thus the most expensive in terms of premiums. As an example of the traps for the unwary, a first-time horse owner may take out a policy and insure his horse at the cheapest rate, thinking he will only be hacking it out and doing a few riding-club show jumping and dressage competitions at weekends. But after a few months he gains in confidence and ambition and decides to go hunting.

Unfortunately his horse has a bad fall and has to be put down. The grieving owner seeks some compensation by claiming for the death and hoping the money will go towards the purchase of a new horse. But he has overlooked informing the insurance company that he wanted to upgrade his equestrian activities and they refuse to settle the claim as the horse was not being used for the purposes agreed at the time the policy was taken out.

Another problem, especially for the person who does not keep his tack at home, can arise over settlement of claims for stolen tack. If you look carefully at the small print on many policies there is usually a clause that states that tack is only covered against theft if it is kept in a permanent building with proper mortice locks or equivalent. (Providing a padlock will not usually satisfy insurance companies that you have taken all reasonable precautions to deter thieves.)

Timber stable yards with integral tack sheds do not always count as 'permanent' and if tack is stolen from this sort of building, or indeed from a horsebox while you are at a show, it is unlikely to be replaced by the insurance company.

If you do not have your own horse-keeping facilities and are worried about security arrangements at your rented premises or livery yard, contact the insurance company and discuss it with them. If you have a good no-claims record and can warrant that you have not suffered any previous tack losses the company may be persuaded to take on the risk even though the security of the building is not as great as they would wish. If they cannot agree to this I would recommend that you keep valuable items at home, inconvenient as it may be to cart saddles back and forth to the yard in your car. As I found to my cost when my own tack room was burgled, although the company reimbursed the purchase price of all my saddlery, it was nothing like enough money to replace everything at today's ever-increasing prices.

It is important to be aware that even if you have not deliberately withheld information about your horse or your own horse insurance history in an attempt to gain cover for an unreasonable risk, the mere fact that you have done so could be enough to prompt the insurance company into invalidating the entire policy. Quite inadvertently you could suddenly find yourself on an insurance 'blacklist', unable to get cover elsewhere except perhaps for a drastically increased premium. Ironically, some companies may accept horses with an 'if' if the owner is absolutely frank at the outset, although they may impose certain exclusions or set a lower limit on the sum reimbursable for claims arising directly from the pre-existing condition. The maxim to follow when filling out an insurance proposal form is 'if in doubt, leave in'.

Additional problems for the part-time horse-keeper or livery owner lie in the fact that his horse does not have guaranteed 24-hour supervision, and thus is more at risk to the repercussions of illness, injury or theft because he could be unwell or missing for hours before help was at hand. It is therefore crucial that you indicate where the horse is kept on the insurance proposal form if the address is different to your own, and also to point out whether or not anyone actually lives on the spot. This way you have alerted the insurer that the horse has only part-time supervision which could stand you in good stead if there is any allegation of contributory negligence in the event of a claim.

Another insurance trap for the unwary livery owner is the use of his horse by others. It is one thing to allow a friend to hack out a horse for you couple of times a week while you are at work, but quite another to allow your horse to be used by a riding school, for financial reward, for student or client lessons. You may try to come to an arrangement with the yard owner about where liability lies in this instance, but even if the yard owner agrees to accept responsibility for any accident your horse has – or causes – while being used by the school, I would still strongly recommend that the insurer is told of the arrangement. Riding-school animals are usually insurable at a premium not grossly higher than privately owned horses. Surely it is best to pay the extra than to have to stand a substantial loss because the horse has been involved in an accident while ridden by someone you don't even know?

Placing a value on a horse is always difficult and sometimes invidious, as in many cases the sum payable for a total loss claim is the 'sum insured, or the market value, whichever is the lesser'; you can rest assured that the insurer will always argue that the horse would have fetched far less on the market than the sum he was originally prepared to take the horse for. If your horse is worth relatively little in the open market it may not be worth insuring him against death or theft; most insurers note that there is a maximum settlement per claim not exceeding the sum insured. For instance, an ordinary cob used for hacking may be insured by his owner for £900 on a policy that also offers veterinary fee reimbursement up to £750 per incident. The horse is seriously ill, incurring veterinary fees of £700, and despite the vet's best efforts it still dies. If the owner is lucky he will receive reimbursement of veterinary fees in full but only £200 against the total loss because the illness and death are regarded as being part of the same incident.

Security

Even if you are well insured, you still don't want to go through the trauma of having your animal stolen. Horse rustling is big business these days. Some horses are stolen to be sold on as pleasure horses but the vast majority, however valuable, invariably end up in sales destined for the meat-market. Organised gangs of horse thieves can have animals up the motorway in the middle of the night and into an abattoir before the owner notices they are missing.

Although there have been cases of stabled animals being stolen in broad daylight from right under their owners' noses, generally speaking horses kept in an isolated field or unsupervised yard away from home are at considerably greater risk, not only to thieves but also to vandals who may find it amusing to let them out or interfere in other ways.

For your own peace of mind you should spend as much time and money as you can afford in improving the security of the premises you use. If the worst does happen, at least you may gain some small comfort from the fact you had done all you could.

Free advice on security is available from your local crime prevention police officer, and there are several companies now specialising in security and alarm systems for livestock accommodation. You certainly do need a system that a horse cannot set off itself by mistake. A friend of mine had this problem and got quite used to the wailing siren going off about twice a week when his horses managed to activate the system. Complacency went too far, however, for one day he strolled down to the stables to switch the thing off and chanced upon daylight intruders already half way across the yard with a barrow full of saddles!

You should not, however, be talked into buying a very sophisticated and expensive system in cases where something simple could have the effect of scaring intruders away. Even if your stables are isolated, thieves who get caught out by, say a floodlight, are highly unlikely to stick around to find out if the place is wired to the main house or police station. Simple but effective lighting devices can be easily and inexpensively rigged up using a car battery and headlamps. Such floodlights could also be used at field gates to surprise and frighten off intruders, although the practicalities may depend on how many people legitimately have access to the field and how likely they are to remember to fix up the circuit breaker when they go.

Certainly anything you can do to waste an intruder's time as he tries to break into buildings or stable yards is worthwhile, though I could not endorse the idea of padlocking each individual stable. Such action could stop help getting to your horse in the event of sudden illness, like colic attacks, or worse still, an outbreak of fire. A guard dog or a guard goose can be useful, but the owners can be liable for any injuries these animals cause, even to trespassers of ill-intent.

Horses kept in fields, especially those away from the house or yard, present rather more of a problem. Ideally the gates should open on to private premises or narrow, one-way cart tracks, rather than on to the main road. This may discourage thieves as a long walk to their waiting lorry is not worth the risk.

A proper metal field gate that cannot be lifted off its hinges is the most secure, with two sets of padlocks and chains where it opens, which will waste just that bit more of the intruder's time. Good stout hedging or solid post and rail is the best fencing in terms of the horse's safety as well as security, because it is time-consuming to cut down. There is no point having a gate secured like Fort Knox if intruders can merely take wire-cutters to the adjacent fence. A ditch along any fence-line, especially where it borders a main road and has no obvious gate, may deter the thief; however willingly the horse may jump a ditch when ridden, it is quite another thing for a stranger to lead him over a spooky hole in the ground in the middle of the night.

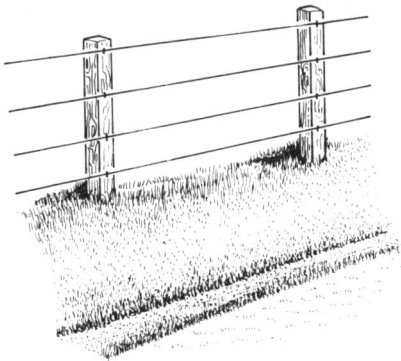

A wide ditch along a fence-line will help to deter thieves where fencing is of a type easily cut.

135

It can be an advantage to have a horse that is difficult to catch (though in making things easier for you to catch him every day, don't make it easier for thieves too by leaving his headcollar on in the field). I once had my horses out with a very strange mare who was so possessive about her 'herd' that she literally fought off any people who tried to get near them. All the owners knew that the answer was to catch her first, when she immediately became all sweetness and light, although this extra chore became a nuisance when we were pushed for time.

It was my firm intention not to 'plug' any particular service or brand name in this book but I would make one exception in strongly recommending everyone, and especially those who live and work away from their animals, to have their horses freeze-marked by Premier FarmKey Ltd of Banbury. They run a national scheme in cooperation with the police network across the UK and with the approval of the BHS. When the scheme was initiated some of the horsy establishment, notably among the showing fraternity, deplored the practice on the trivial grounds that the brand marks would detract from the horse's appearance and encourage the judge to put them down the line. Having spoken to several distraught victims who attribute the loss of their animals to failing to join the FarmKey scheme, I can hardly see how the disappointment of losing a class under a prejudiced judge can possibly compare with the heartache of knowing that somewhere your horse is hanging up on a butcher's hook.

For a relatively inexpensive fee (discounts are offered for group bookings), a trained operator from FarmKey imprints a personal code (currently a combination of four letters and numbers) on the horse, usually under the saddle area. Chemically frozen irons, without pain or discomfort, kill the pigmentation cells in the skin, so that when the hair regrows – usually within six weeks – it comes up white, showing the code clearly. With grey horses, the irons are held on long enough to kill the hair follicles so that the numbers show as bare skin. A saddle normally only has to be kept off the horse's back for five days to a week as a precaution to prevent soreness before normal riding can resume. Sometimes the number can be put on the shoulder, flank or neck though these areas are more difficult to mark clearly.

In the event of theft, FarmKey immediately alerts the police, slaughterhouses, sales and markets with the number and description of the horse. The incentive for the meat-man, auctioneer or other parties to cooperate is a reward of up to £2,000 for information leading to the safe return of the animal – some four or five times greater than the carcass value. To date, FarmKey has a 100 per cent success rate in securing the safe return of stolen freeze-marked horses, but the deterrent effect is equally important. I have heard of cases where a large field's worth of horses has disappeared into the night, except for the one or two animals who were freeze-marked. FarmKey can provide effective stickers and plaques for stables and field gates, and also fabric badges for rugs which state, *'Warning, this horse is freeze-marked and can be identified by the police.'*

FarmKey also runs a similar tack security system, again supplying you with a personal code number on a pair of specially tipped pliers with which you can mark every last saddle flap and strap. Most county constabularies, recognising the increasing problem of tack thefts, regularly offer free tack marking, imprinting your saddlery with your post code. The value of this is more limited, however, because there is always the chance the thief has nearly the same post code as your own. Two months after my tack was stolen the police asked me to identify a hoard of stolen saddles found in a house only half a mile away.

Saddlery security presents a real problem for those who keep horses away from home. These days I tend to keep everything at the yard (rugs, boots and bandages pose less of a security risk because they have a very low secondhand value), except my saddles which are kept in the house. Having to cart them back and forth in the hatchback is a minor inconvenience that I am prepared to put up with.

Whether or not you have your horse freeze-marked, you should prepare for theft by having identification documents and photographs readily to hand for distribution to the police and other agencies who may help you, like the Horses and Ponies Protection Association, who run a lost and found register.

If you have your horse regularly vaccinated against tetanus and equine 'flu the chances are that you already have a detailed certificate on which the horse's distinguishing marks – shape of blaze, socks, scars and whorls, etc. – have been noted and verified by a vet. Alternatively, or in addition, get several sets of colour photographs of your horse, both in his winter and summer coat and also when clipped out (in each instance he can look quite different), from either side, front and rear. If possible, take close-ups of the horse's chestnuts which are as unique to him as fingerprints are to us. These 'portfolios' should be passed to your yard manager or landlord, or any one else responsible for your horse in your absence. I may sound alarmist but you cannot afford to waste even half an hour when a theft is spotted, for horse rustlers move like lightning.

The BHS will supply, for the cost of an SAE, an updated pamphlet giving names, address and 'phone numbers of abattoirs and horse sales nationwide. When you get it, spend a few minutes checking the days on which sales are held, and mark the locations of slaughterhouses and markets within driving distance on your road map to avoid wasting valuable time if the worst should happen.

The police will usually alert the local press and specialist magazines. Horses have indeed been recovered as a direct result of being spotted by sharp-eyed readers of *Horse and Hound*, but on the whole this publicity, though always given willingly, has a limited value. There may be a lapse of several days if not a week between its going to press and hitting the news stands. Local TV and radio can offer immediate publicity but you should be prepared for the news editors to turn down your request if the 'news value' does not compare with the other stories fighting for space on their bulletins.

As a general precaution, there is no harm in asking the police if your isolated field or stables can be included in night patrols, and ask your neighbours to keep an eye open for any suspicious persons they see around the place in your absence.

Appendix 1

Timetables

The following are specimen timetables I have managed to work to over the past twelve years when keeping horses part-stabled at premises away from my home, either in livery yards or rented accommodation where I have no other help. All times are approximate and are offered merely as an indication, and I would not presume to suggest they are ideal.

Timetable A

Stabled horse, turned out all day, one visit before work from owner daily. Evening chores, feeds and rugging done by livery yard or other staff.

6.45 Arrive yard, inspect horse for any signs of injury from previous day or night.
6.50 Remove obvious piles of droppings.
6.55 Brush off, giving principal attention to head, saddle patch, girth, between elbows and lower leg between knee/hock and coronet band; pick out feet.
7.08 Tack up.
7.15-8.02 Ride.
8.03 Untack, wash off bit in water bucket, use same to sponge off head and saddle patch if necessary.
8.10 Tie up by manger; rug up for field as required and feed breakfast.
8.13 Leave horse in peace to enjoy breakfast and prepare feeds and haynets for rest of day; and leave them where yard staff know where to find them.
8.20-35 Leave horse tied up and muck out.
8.36-38 Empty barrow.
8.38 Empty water bucket/s and replace with fresh water.

8.40 Turn out in field for day.

8.45 Change and leave for work.

Timetable B

Stabled horse, turned out daytime by yard, two visits daily by owner, before and after work.

MORNING VISIT

7.15 Arrive at yard.

7.18-7.23 Remove obvious piles of droppings.

7.24-7.31 Tack up.

7.32-8.12 Ride.

8.13 Untack, wash off bit in water bucket, use same water to sponge off saddle patch and head, if necessary, and damp mane.

8.20 Tidy up horse, rug up for field as required and feed small section of hay to keep horse amused.

8.25-8.35 Leave horse tied up, complete mucking out.

8.36-8.38 Empty barrow.

8.39 Empty last night's water bucket/s and replace with fresh water.

8.42 Untie horse, feed breakfast and leave him to eat in peace.

8.45 Change and leave for work.

EVENING VISIT

6.30 Arrive at yard. Inspect horse for any cuts etc. sustained in field and wash or brush mud off legs if this has not been done.

6.34-6.39 Give late feed if needed and prepare all tomorrow's feeds and haynets and leave them where yard can find them.

6.40-6.50 Skip out box, put banks up and add bedding if required.

6.51-7.01 Reset or replace rugs, deftly brush off horse concentrating on head, saddle patch, girth area and between forelegs.

7.02-7.06 Top up water buckets and hay as required. Leave yard.

Appendix 2

Tethering

Here is a summary of the code of practice for tethering produced by the National Equine Welfare Committee and the RSPCA:

SITE   Should be well grassed, especially if grass is going to be the sole source of food, and free from poisonous plants. It should be reasonably flat, offer an area of shade. It should not cross a public foot path or be close to a road or other public highway. It should not be waterlogged and there should be no object or projections within the radius of the tether round which the horse could become entangled. The tether must not permit the animal to come into contact with wire or other fences. The site must be of at least a 20 ft (6 m) radius.

TYPES OF TETHER   Both the leather neck band or the leather headcollar must be fitted with a swivel. The tethering line must be firmly staked, the chain must be of an appropriate weight for the animal concerned. It should be attached to the stake with a 360-degree swivel fitting at ground level which allows the pony to move in a complete circle without tangling the tether.

AGE AND CONDITION OF HORSES   Horses and ponies less than two years old must not normally be tethered. Mares in season must not be tethered near stallions. Mares about to foal must not be tethered.

WATER   Clean water must be available at all times in troughs or containers that are securely placed and not easily upset.

INSPECTION   Tethered animals should be visited at least twice every 24 hours.

CHANGING OF SITE   This must depend on the ground, the size and type of pony but should be changed every 24 hours if the grass is the sole source of food.

WIND   If no natural protection is available some form of artificial windbreak is essential.

Index